Landscape Archaeology and Ecology Special Series

Papers from the Landscape
Conservation Forum

*Volume (3) A. Wild by Design
and
B. Ploughing on Regardless*

Ian D. Rotherham and Christine Handley (eds.)

August 2012

Edited by Ian D. Rotherham and Christine Handley

ISBN 978-1-904098-39-3

Published by:
Wildtrack Publishing, Venture House,
103 Arundel Street, Sheffield S1 2NT

Typeset and processed by Christine Handley

Supported by:
Biodiversity and Landscape History Research Institute.
Sheffield Hallam University.
HEC Associates Ltd.

© Wildtrack Publishing and the individual authors

All rights reserved. No part of this publication may be reproduced or transmitted in any form or by any means, electronic or mechanical, including photocopying, recording, or any information storage or retrieval system, without permission in writing from the publisher.

CONTENTS

A. WILD BY DESIGN

INTRODUCTION — 1

LANDSCAPE CHANGE AND THE FUTURE OF AGRICULTURE AND FORESTRY: THE CONTEXT OF WILDER AREAS
Tom Oliver — 3

A REGIONAL BIODIVERSITY AUDIT FOR YORKSHIRE AND THE HUMBER
Kevin Bayes — 12

MANAGING WOODLANDS IN THE UK - THE RELEVANCE OF THE WILDERNESS APPROACH
George Peterken — 17

THE DYNAMIC INFLUENCE OF HISTORY AND ECOLOGY ON THE RESTORATION OF A MAJOR URBAN HEATHLAND AT WHARNCLIFFE, SOUTH YORKSHIRE
Ian D. Rotherham, John C. Rose and Chris Percy — 22

B. PLOUGHING ON REGARDLESS

INTRODUCTION — 37

THE EFFECTS OF PLOUGHING ON ANCIENT TREES
Ted Green — 39

PLOUGHING, PARTICIPATION AND PARTNERS: AGRI-ENVIRONMENT SCHEMES AND ARABLE ARCHAEOLOGY
Bob Middleton — 41

FARMING WITH HERITAGE - THE PRACTICALITIES
John Seymour — 46

FARMLAND FLOWERS – THE IMPORTANCE OF CULTIVATION
Martin Harper — 48

WILDING BY DESIGN AS A FUTURE DRIVER FOR A NEW NATURE IN RECONSTRUCTING SOUTH YORKSHIURE'S FENS
Ian D. Rotherham and Keith Harrison — 54

Landscape Archaeology and Ecology Special Series - Landscape Conservation Forum: Wild by Design & Ploughing On, August 2012

Wild by Design?
- managing landscape change:
Introduction

Organised by **The Landscape Conservation Forum**, this event was aimed at all those involved in the conservation of sites and landscapes. It intended to address critical issues of landscape management and landscape change. These include how agricultural, urban and post-industrial landscapes change and evolve. It considered the impacts of agricultural diversification and extensification, and issues such as managed retreat from coastal and floodplain zones, as well as proposals for the release of upland areas from pastoral grazing management.

What are the implications for the historic environment – for sites, monuments and the historic landscape? How do ideas of wilderness and natural landscapes impact on wildlife, the landscape itself, and for the people that live and work there?

What do we mean or even understand by the idea of wild or natural landscapes? In the same context, how can an understanding of landscape evolution help to inform the decisions that inform the current suite of changes?

Speakers and participants included landscape professionals, archaeologists, ecologists, earth scientists, planners, conservationists and those in education. They brought to the event a diversity and wealth of experience from the UK, across Europe and indeed from around the world. As always it was an enjoyable and informative day with chance for wide-ranging discussion amongst delegates and speakers.

Programme

Introduction and welcome: Dr Ian D. Rotherham Sheffield Hallam University and Chair of the Landscape Conservation Forum.

Morning Session Chair: Ken Smith Peak National Park Authority.

Tom Oliver, Council for National Parks: *Landscape change and the future of agriculture and forestry: the context of Wilder Areas*

Professor Peter Fowler, World Heritage consultant: *Landscape by design*

Sophie Milner, National Trust, and Albyn Smith, Forestry Commission: *The Alport Valley: a practical example of wilder by design*

Kevin Bayes, RSPB: *Futurescapes: landscape change – the RSPB view*

Afternoon Session: Chair:

Dave Batchelor and Amanda Chadburn, English Heritage: *Stonehenge: landscape in transition?*

Dr John Pygott, Environment Agency: *Planning for the Rising Tides - the Humber Estuary Shoreline Management Plan - delivering managed retreat over the next five years?*

Dr George Peterken: *Managing woodlands in the UK the relevance of the wilderness approach*

Discussion and Concluding remarks: Dr Ian D. Rotherham, Chair, Landscape Conservation Forum.

LANDSCAPE CHANGE AND THE FUTURE OF AGRICULTURE AND FORESTRY: THE CONTEXT OF WILDER AREAS

Tom Oliver
Council for National Parks.

INTRODUCTION

This paper reviews the *Wilder Areas Initiative* of 1997 and places it in the context of agricultural and land management changes since. The paper appraises the present influences on farming and landscape in National Parks in particular and discusses the emerging circumstances faced in National Parks and some of the wider issues raised by the idea of wilder areas. The Council for National Parks (CNP) is the national charity that works to protect and enhance the National Parks and areas which merit National Park status and to promote understanding and quiet enjoyment of National Parks for the benefit of all.

National Park statutory purposes are set out in *Section 61* of the *Environment Act 1995* and are:

- The conservation and enhancement of natural beauty, wildlife and cultural heritage; and

- The promotion of opportunities for the public understanding and enjoyment of the special qualities of the National Park.

Within the first purpose of National Parks, the significance of enhancement is emphasised in the case of the subject under discussion. The importance of understanding the relationship between conservation and enhancement is also evident.

In order to be clear about the status and the nature of National Parks in England and Wales, it is helpful to refer to the *Edwards Report*, the Report of the National Parks Review Panel, 1991. In Chapter 17 this sets out the distinction between National Parks and protected landscapes as set out by the *International Union for Conservation of Nature and National Resources* (IUCN). The National Parks of England and Wales come within what is known as Category V in the IUCN system; they are areas which are a *"product of the harmonious interaction of people and nature"* rather than being a *"relatively large natural area"* owned by the state and by and large uninfluenced by long term human activity within the bounds of the designated area. Our National Parks, like our other landscapes, have millennia of human influence written across them and this influence will continue into the foreseeable future.

This paper sets out to review some of the background to the various initiatives in this field, to put the subject into a general policy context and briefly to consider examples of work presently underway. This paper deals specifically with National Parks, but looks towards the connections between work in National Parks and the wider landscape. The paper provides a short analysis of the idea of wilder areas and the various aspects of the processes involved and what the future may hold in the most general terms. Lastly, this paper considers some of the difficulties with the concept of wilder areas, wilder landscapes and wildness and draws attention to some recurrent but important points of debate.

WILD BY DESIGN

In 1997, the Council for National Parks published a report *Wild by Design* supported by the then DoE Environmental Action Fund and the Dennis Curry Charitable Trust. The report "*set out to consider how the creation of wilder areas might be taken forward*" and made four key recommendations: the encouragement of debate and dialogue on the question of wilder areas; the establishment of a pilot scheme for a large area to be returned to "*near natural condition*"; the encouragement of smaller schemes for the enhancement of semi natural landscapes and work on the definition of the role of National Park Authorities in taking the wilder areas initiative forward. A continued programme of lobbying and seminar discussion was suggested.

Since 1997, there have been substantial changes in the way agriculture and rural land management are regarded and how each is expected to develop in the future. At a global scale, world trade negotiations have moved towards freer markets, where subsidy for agricultural production is steadily reduced. Within Europe, the planned expansion of the EU may yet force change in the short term, as spelt out in the Mid Term Review (MTR). Huge changes to European funding of agriculture so long predicted, are still thoroughly entangled in the higher politics of the Council of Europe, but the political pressure to reform agricultural expenditure in many EU states will do anything but diminish. At a national level, the long established ministerial regime which supported agriculture and insulated it from serious change has been swept away and the power now exercised on behalf of the rural economy is greatly diminished. Deadlock across the EU may precipitate more independent action by northern European states. Ironically enough, resistance to change comes from southern European states which are experiencing re-wilding on a vast and unmanaged scale in marginal agricultural landscapes. While southern European states fight a rearguard action against re-wilding, some northern states wait impatiently for EU funds to help initiate the very same process.

In Britain, changes in rural society, again so long discussed, are now upon us. The average age of farmers is reaching the retirement threshold and the will of the next generation to take on the way of life which has run the landscape for the last fifty years appears to have all but collapsed. The impact of specific catastrophes, including BSE and FMD has hastened the process, but the momentum of change shows no sign of slowing.

At the same time, significant positive and creative developments have emerged. The CROW Act has offered the prospect of improved enjoyment of the countryside and better protection of designated sites. The new ministry, DEFRA, has within it elements which have grasped the challenge of sustainability and huge change. Government Agencies, such as the Forestry Commission, have shown vision in their internal reviews and policies and the Government has responded positively to the Curry Report in the wake of FMD with an encouraging settlement in the CSR. There is a prospect of real improvement in the delivery of agricultural support, through internal review by DEFRA (Broad and Shallow and Tir Gofal in Wales) and the measures proposed in the MTR (the decoupling of subsidies and production, increased modulation, cross compliance to ensure basic environmental standards and farm audits). Some of these need not wait for the rest of the EU and we should anticipate them.

NGOs have also shown inspiring leadership and the ability to form effective partnerships with government agencies. Reports such as *"The New Wildwoods Project"*, the Hills Task Force Report and the RSPB *"Futurescapes"* proposals are examples of the creative thinking which has taken place, while projects such as Whitelee Moor in Northumberland and Cwm Idwal in Snowdonia are attempts to pursue significant change in land management in order to achieve noticeably wilder landscapes.

At Whitelee, the Northumberland Wildlife Trust is managing 1,510 hectares, of which a very small proportion, 35 hectares is being replanted with *"new natural woodland"*. At Holystone Valley, the NWT is also responsible for managing a site which may contain the last stand of native English *Pinus sylvestris*. At Kielderhead, the NWT is managing a complex of 4,500 hectares of border mire, which has involved some removal of plantations and the reversal of extensive drainage for forestry.

At Cwm Idwal, the first fruit of the new management regime has been the rediscovery and possibly the saving of the Snowdon hawkweed (*Hieracium Snowdoniense*).

At the very least, therefore, the time has come to take stock of the changes that have taken place since the publication of *Wild By Design* and to evaluate the effects on National Parks and elsewhere of the processes influencing agricultural change. This paper proposes further that the significance of the changes now underway, the threats posed to much of what has hitherto been identified as being central to the identity of National Parks and other protected landscapes and the opportunities to secure beneficial change through careful planning and cooperation, make renewed and more extensive attention to land management issues an urgent consideration. The 1997 document identifies the crucial importance of the integration of policy approaches and the work of individual organisations to success in progress with wilder area initiatives. It also outlined the leading role that National Park Authorities might play in such work.

NATIONAL PARKS

The *Edwards Report* in 1991, in Chapter Six, devoted to farming in National Parks, suggested *"that, for conservation reasons, certain areas should be allowed to develop a natural succession of vegetation"*. The Report suggested a first experimental phase and put forward criteria that each project should satisfy: enhancement of the landscape and wildlife conservation; physical self-containment; to be distant from major recreation areas and to avoid inconveniencing neighbouring agricultural enterprises.

The Review of English National Parks Authorities of 2002 contains several recommendations which offer the opportunity to take this role forward. These include *Recommendation 8* which champions pilot schemes to *"test ways of better integrating land management with protecting and enhancing the landscape and biodiversity"* and *"to enable some areas to revert to a more wild state"*. Other recommendations that are relevant include *Recommendations 6* and *7* which deal with the application of agri-environment schemes and *Recommendation 9* which deals with the monitoring of the condition and status of habitats and species. It is evident that all these recommendations are in the realm of careful, measured and often intensive intervention and management.

The changes that have taken place since 1997 have redoubled the degree of uncertainty in the farming industry, weakened the ability of farmers to take initiatives within the realm of conventional farming and left the way open for an increasing variety of outside influences which may or may not be harmonious with the qualities presently valued in National Parks.

At the same time, all parties involved in protection and enhancement of existing valuable landscape, habitat and monuments are rightly concentrating on sustaining their management practices in the face of change.

This paper assumes that whatever the degree of change, the actual outcome of the agriculture or land management taking place in National Parks will be at the core of the delivery of National Park purposes. Two key questions can be asked:

1. Is there a significant need for initiatives addressing the scale of change in agriculture and forestry in National Parks?

2. Should consideration of changes in agriculture be divided into two separate issues, of *"conventional"* agri-environmental measures

within the context of present farming activity on the one hand and wilder landscape initiatives on the other?

The scale of change set out in the introduction suggests that the forces at work upon National Parks are at least as strong as those which acted to damage so much of the semi natural landscape between 1945 and the 1980s. Rapid changes in circumstances are likely to undermine the processes which have sustained National Park landscapes, communities and characteristics. The vulnerable fabric of traditional farming practice and the possibilities for radical change in land management are equally subject to the course of events. National Park purposes will surely be well served by careful anticipation, planning and management of these changes. There is a valuable role to be undertaken in influencing the strategic policy framework which will eventually determine the long term future of the Parks.

The scale of change and the threats to the survival of traditional farm practices, businesses and infrastructure indicate that the future of land management in National Parks is tending towards more fragmented, diverse and unpredictable outcomes. The ownership and use of agricultural and open land is changing fast as the pressures on farming are compounded by increasing prosperity in parts of the urban economy.

Positive responses to the changes taking place have been very varied indeed. A spectrum of vision and initiative is evident, from modest changes in the extent of *Environmentally Sensitive Areas* and *Countryside Stewardship Schemes*, through the ambitious and thoroughly researched Futurescapes proposals of the RSPB for habitat recovery and creation, to the *"near natural"* initiatives in Snowdonia and Northumberland. It is clear that there is no satisfactory way to categorise such initiatives; any attempt to do so can be countered or questioned. *"Self conscious"* land management can have a very varied set of objectives.

The concept of wilder areas has always met with criticism from some quarters, mainly on social and economic grounds and an uncertainty over the value placed on cultural heritage by a vision of a wilder environment. Furthermore, debate over what constitutes action to create a wilder landscape, the great questions of extent, intensity or absence of management, timescale and the effects of alien species and climate change all combine to cloud the debate or divide the consideration of initiatives into different quarters. The decline of agriculture in the 1920s and 1930s was a great re-wilding exercise, as was that of 1870s before it. In each case, extensification often verged upon total abandonment with devastating consequences for local economies and communities.

Meanwhile, the understanding of the potential for wide-scale land management change is rapidly increasing. Some of this work is inspired by an approach close to the *"near natural"* vision of *Wild by Design*, while other projects are working with the grain of the existing farming and woodland regime, with an objective of biological, landscape and access enhancement. There is genuine debate as to the virtues of these different approaches found in different places on the wide spectrum described.

Two ideas can be seen to link all this often bewildering variety together. First is the key land management question of scale: scale of change; extent of land affected; time scale for the achievement of objectives; the range of responses which are possible and the impact on the social and economic fabric of such change.

Consideration of scale must be matched with the vital importance of integration of activity or the lack of it, by all parties. The National Park Authorities, especially following the changes indicated in the recent Review, are well placed to be leaders and facilitators in policy and practical management work. This role has already been emphasised in *Paragraph 18* of *Circular 12/96 (Department of the Environment)*: National Parks can be *"models for the sustainable management of the wider countryside"*. But clearly, other organisations, Wildlife Trusts, the National Trust, private owners and even the MoD have their vital role to play in the pursuit of National Park purposes in this time of uncertainty and change. The importance of new Regional Government structures in taking forward rural development initiatives should also be anticipated as should be the ability of Regional Government to secure resources in the longer-term.

The range of responses and potential responses to change is thus so wide and the number of potential stakeholders so great, that it is wise to approach long term landscape initiatives in as inclusive a way as possible. Whether characterised as *"wilder"* or as *"enhanced"*, the benefits to National Park landscapes and other protected landscapes might be vast.

One thing that is evident from a brief review of the wilder areas literature of the last decade or so is the relative lack of development in thought over that time. The excellent observations made in the Countryside Commission's Conference of March 1990 are almost identical to those of Farquhar and Pennington as set out this year in the *North Yorkshire Moors Association Magazine*. The work of CNP in the late 1990s, concentrated minds and set objectives, but the various practitioners have pursued their different paths since. There is a need to ensure that those involved in National Parks act as stimulators, challengers, advocates and co-ordinators of new thinking, working closely with National Park Authorities as they respond to the opportunities which arise for positive change.

The *Joint Statement on Nature Conservation in the National Parks* between ANPA and English Nature of 22 September 2000 includes support for the testing of experimental schemes related to rural land and water management, as well as the achieving of UK BAP priorities. This experimental role for National Park Authorities will be pivotal in progress made in land management in the foreseeable future. Further, the National Parks Review of July 2002 sets out a vision for National Park Authorities as leaders in best practice, taking the sorts of initiatives which landscapes of national importance should merit. For the first time this year, National Park Officers are contributing directly to DEFRA plans for landscape proposals in National Parks. There is a great opportunity for National Park Authorities to benefit from the wide range of work each will undertake through the sharing of best practice and learning through experience.

Under the *Environment Act 1995*, National Park Authorities are required to prepare National Park Management Plans, reviewed every five years. These Plans may include inventories of Park resources, and are supported by annual State of the Park reports, recording the condition of the Park environment. There are thus clear means of recording the development and outcome of policies designed to achieve wilder characteristics within National Parks. Assembling of information and the recording of experience and its dissemination to wider audiences, as undertaken in 1997 by CNP, would be a logical extension of this work.

There is, of course, no guarantee that the support framework of existing and planned agri-environmental schemes will endure and a great deal of pressure, already outlined, for it to decline or cease altogether. Another significant element in making progress with adaptation to change will be the influencing of national and possibly European policy development. Agri-environmental policy within the context of the existing farming regime is excellently covered by other NGOs but there is a distinct role for the steering of policy towards wider objectives in an era after direct farm support has withered away. National Parks in particular need to have their interests articulated in the policy arena. This is vital in the long term if the huge and diverse possibilities for land management change are to be sustainable and compatible with National Park purposes.

The future "*consumption*" of National Park landscape, the ability of such landscape to pay for itself, and the compatibility of such consumption in the future with what is valuable in National Parks today, requires considerable thought and discussion. The understanding of what might be achieved in the future, with great change in rural communities, agricultural support systems, land ownership and the expectations of the public is still at an early stage. There is merit in considering a role challenging accepted definitions, analysing current objectives and encouraging consideration of new understanding of how land in National Parks could and should be managed.

There are a number of difficult issues which inhabit the conceptual territory of landscape change and wilder areas. It is vital to the long term credibility and success of initiatives in the name of wilder landscapes that these are clearly understood by all concerned. The first is the vast variation in the timescales of different sorts of extensification objectives. The recovery of a pre Industrial Revolution semi natural landscape involves perhaps one or two oak life spans or ten generations of fences. The recovery of a landscape from the Atlantic period, 5,000 years ago, might involve ten oak life spans or 150 generations of fences. If an ancient landscape is intended, exactly how ancient should it be? This makes a great difference to the preferred outcome. And is it possible to consider a previous period without its contemporary climate or divorced from what is happening in the world around it? It matters to be clear about this, as otherwise anything goes in what could amount to a futurist free style.

The second is the reality of political, social and economic continuity over the sorts of timescales involved. Can we contemplate a legitimate objective in terms of landscape appearance which will take more than a generation, let alone the span of a term of government, or a Management Plan, to achieve?

The third is the impact of events in the future from new alien introductions to the uncertainties of climate change induced by mankind. Climate change has happened repeatedly without human agency and alien species are abroad in National Parks in large numbers already, but what of human influence as yet unknown? How legitimate might such changes make a wilder or "*near natural*" landscape of the future?

CONCLUSIONS

None of these issues is unfamiliar and none prevents serious contemplation and creation of wilder landscapes. But there needs to be constant clarity amongst all concerned with this great enterprise. In the immediate future, there are some useful jobs to be done. They include:

- Close involvement with and support for the development of landscape policy by National Park Authorities by other parties;

- Monitoring of the range of projects and initiatives underway or planned which promise to point the way for wholesale change in the future;

- Effective engagement with stakeholders;

- Long term advocacy in the policy arena of the interests of National Parks, other protected landscapes and their communities beyond the era of direct agricultural support;

- Development of a well informed and documented overview of the developments in land management in National Parks for the benefit of all stakeholders.

- The Government has put sustainability closer still to the heart of policy in the wake of Johannesburg. There is an important role for wilder landscapes in delivering the sustainable future which is universally sought.

REFERENCES

DEFRA (2002) *Review of English National Park Authorities*, DEFRA, p18

A REGIONAL BIODIVERSITY AUDIT FOR YORKSHIRE AND THE HUMBER

Kevin Bayes
Senior Conservation Officer, RSPB

INTRODUCTION

A *Biodiversity Audit for Yorkshire and the Humber* was published and officially launched in December 1999. That was the culmination of two years work. The project officers Richard Selman and Felicité Dodd undertook nine person-months of intense activity sifting and collating thousands of pieces of information to create the wildlife jigsaw called the audit. A further four months of editing and polishing the text was necessary to complete the document. Though the work was carried out and managed by the RSPB, it was undertaken on behalf of the *Yorkshire and Humber Regional Biodiversity Forum*.

The Audit project drew heavily upon the national biodiversity guidance issued by national Government. It essentially asked two questions. What relevance does the national biodiversity process have for this Region and, what can this Region best contribute to national biodiversity action? Those key species from the national 'short and medium' lists which occur in the Region and those habitats on the UK Priority habitats list which are present in the Region were the starting point for the audit. No attempt was made to define or identify other species or habitats which are important in a Regional context but which do not appear on the national lists. That work is progressing now and will be published in due course as an addendum to the original volume. Concentrating on the national lists kept the initial project to a manageable size and has arguably identified the essential core for conservation action within the Region.

THE REGIONAL AUDIT

More than sixty wildlife specialists contributed information and expertise to the document. Some of these people are employed by statutory agencies and local authorities, but most of them are amateurs, in the true sense of the word, devoting time freely to a subject they love. In some instances, the project officers were granted access to a lifetimes worth of information and it is important to recognise that without the support and generosity of these people, the audit would not have been possible.

For the first time, this project has pulled together all of the available information on the key species and habitats of the Region. It presents those data in a logical and consistent format. The survey quantifies amounts of habitats by pooling information from a variety of sources and provides distributions of key habitats and species as well as information on ecology, management and threats. Yorkshire and the Humber is a large Region, stretching from the North Sea and the Humber Estuary in the east to the high moors of the Pennines in the west. It is perhaps unsurprising, given that geographic and altitudinal variation, that the Region enjoys one of the finest arrays of wildlife habitats. Thirty-five national priority habitats occur in the Region, including 52% of the UK's limestone pavement, 28% of England's upland heath, 20% of UK calcareous grassland, 16% of UK upland hay meadows and 11.5% of GB saline lagoons. Perhaps the most obscure of the habitats are the natural reefs off the Yorkshire coast formed by agglomeration of the calcareous tubes produced by the marine tubeworm *Sabularia spinulosa*. Within the main audit document there are details of all thirty-five habitats. The level of detail is totally dependent on the amount of information available. Where possible, habitat areas have been quantified. The habitat distributions are shown on maps, presenting information according to local planning authority boundaries and in comparison to English Nature's Natural Areas.

From a great trawl of species records, a total of 173 species was considered; of these eighty-four have been recorded reliably in the Region in the last ten years. A further twenty-one are probably still present but have not been recorded recently. Sixty-seven species were formerly present but are now almost certainly extinct within the Region. One record was impossible to categorise.

A few species highlights include:

- Yorkshire feather moss *Thamnobryum cataractarum* endemic to the Region;
- A Lady's Mantle species *Alchemilla minima* endemic to the Region;
- A ground beetle *Bembidion humerale*, in Britain, only known from Thorne, Crowle and Hatfield Moors;
- The Mire Pill Beetle *Curimopsis nigritta*, with only three known British sites, all within this Region;
- Nowell's limestone moss *Zygodon gracilis* - the only known UK site is within this Region;
- Lady's slipper orchid *Cypripedium calceolus* - the UK's only natural population is within this Region.

REGIONAL BIODIVERSITY CONSERVATION

Whilst the audit is a significant achievement in its own right, providing baseline information on biodiversity for the Region, it should be considered as an integral part of a much wider process which will ultimately dramatically improve biodiversity conservation in the Region.

The project set out with clear aims, many of which have been achieved. Critical amongst these was recognition of the need to provide suitable information on biodiversity to feed into the crucial 'strategic plans' for the Region. These are currently being developed. Key findings already appear in the draft revised *Regional Planning Guidance* which informs all land-use planning. Audit information was used in the drawing up of the *Rural Development Plan* which informs agricultural and other rural development issues. Audit information will feature in the *Regional Sustainable Development Framework* document. A number of key audiences for the audits findings, identified at the outset, became willing partners and co-funders of the project, a testament to the value of the project. *Yorkshire Forward* (the Regional Development Agency - responsible for improving employment and the Regional economy), the *Regional Chamber* (a partnership of local authorities and other key Regional stakeholders) and the Government Office for the Region (national Government's local presence) will all be involved in making important decisions and devising Regional policy which will, either directly or indirectly, affect the Region's wildlife. There is an important continuing role in helping these major organisations to translate the audit's findings into tangible biodiversity benefit.

A CASE IN POINT: THE HUMBER ESTUARY

Despite being funders of the audit project, *Yorkshire Forward* have not yet fully embraced the importance of biodiversity in the Region and there are examples of biodiversity continuing to be viewed as a potential threat to economic activity. Nowhere can this be seen more clearly than on the Humber Estuary. The estuary holds over 12,000 ha of intertidal muds and sands composed of sediments derived from the rivers which flow into it, which drain one fifth of England and from the sea, much originating from the eroding Holderness coast. These flats team with invertebrate life which in turn support important nurseries for young fish, particularly plaice and sole and at low tide attract large numbers of migrating birds. Around 170,000 wildfowl and waders are recorded from the estuary during peak winter counts. Twelve percent of Europe's knot winter on the Humber, along with eight other internationally important populations. There are nationally and internationally important breeding bird populations too. The avocet here is in its most northerly breeding site in Britain. The Humber population is the fastest growing in the country now and over 120 chicks were raised during the 2000 breeding season.

The Humber is important for a number of other key habitats including saltmarsh, sand dunes, coastal vegetated shingle and saline lagoons. The lagoons in particular are an incredibly scarce habitat holding such bizarre creatures as the tentacled lagoon worm *Alkmaria romijni* and the strange stone-like plant - spiral tasselweed *Ruppia cirrhosa*. The Humber has 150 ha of lagoon habitat out of a UK total of less than 1,300 ha.

This amalgamation of key habitats around the estuary make it one of the most exceptional sites for biodiversity in the Region, but the future of the Humber presents a unique and complex planning challenge. How is it possible to integrate the suite of important land uses around the estuary in a sustainable way? The estuary, its ports and its industrial hinterland are rightly seen as one of the great economic powerhouses of the Region. Until now there has been an uneasy coexistence between the great industries and the fabulous biodiversity value of the adjacent habitats. But pressure on the remaining habitats is increasing. Plans are being developed for a massive increase in industrial activity around the estuary. The *Regional Economic Strategy* has put forward proposals for a *Humber Enterprise Zone*. To date there has been very limited consultation over this matter with conservation organisations. If the zone is planned carefully and sympathetically it will be possible to have industry and biodiversity working in harmony. If the planning is weak and unsustainable, economic growth could be at the cost of Regional quality of life, in terms of lost wildlife habitat.

THE CHALLENGE OF EFFECTIVE COLLABORATIONS

There is clearly a need to build more positive and collaborative partnerships between the environment and economic sectors within the Region if biodiversity is to get the treatment it deserves. There are a number of other obvious generic tasks, including:

- Creation of a list of Regionally important habitats and species to be published as an addendum to the current audit;

- To support the continuing creation of a network of local biodiversity action plans for the Region. Many of these Local Plans are already in place or well on the way to completion. They are the product of an enormous amount of hard work by local committed groups and are or will be the key mechanism by which Biodiversity Planning gets translated onto the ground. None of the activity at Regional level will duplicate or usurp these plans. The audit is an overview to inform, not a replacement plan;

- The protection and sensitive management of key habitats and species;

- To support partnerships to foster education for sustainable development and joint actions for biodiversity;

- To support better acquisition and use of biodiversity information. There is a clear need for coordination of data capture and storage across the Region and a great deal of current work is addressing this.

The critical nature of biodiversity conservation is encapsulated by the former Deputy Prime Minister John Prescott in his foreword to the audit:

"Conserving and enhancing our natural resources is essential to sustainable development and a better quality of life for everyone. The interaction between our everyday activities and the natural world is so pronounced that we can no longer ignore the human impact on the species and habitats around us. Conserving biodiversity can no longer be seen as an add on but should be central to all our thinking and planning for a more sustainable lifestyle. An attractive natural environment can encourage inward investment, help regenerate our towns and cities, and is important to the revival of rural areas."

Conservation of biodiversity is essential for the environment, important to the public and is good for business. And since, once lost species can never be replaced, the conservation of biodiversity is a key test of sustainability. The full Biodiversity Audit and a Public Summary, produced in poster format, are available from Natural England (formerly English Nature) and the RSPB.

MANAGING WOODLANDS IN THE UK - THE RELEVANCE OF THE WILDERNESS APPROACH

George F. Peterken

INTRODUCTION

Foresters rarely talk about wilderness and perhaps few think of it as a factor in their work. The *ruison d'être* of forestry is to manage, not leave land untouched, and few would admit to being disorientated in wild territory, both hallmarks of wilderness. Much the same could be said of nature conservationists.

Furthermore, the history and current state of UK forests and woods militate against forested wilderness. The UK would naturally be almost covered in forest, but much of the original forest was cleared in prehistoric times, and by the late nineteenth century forest cover had shrunk to about 4-5% of the land area. Since then forest has expanded to occupy 11% of the land, and it is still increasing, but this proportion is well short of the European norm. Moreover, the remnants of the original forests survive as a scatter of mostly small woods that have been exploited or managed for millennia, and most of the new forests are plantations dominated by introduced evergreen coniferous tree species that were established to yield timber on short-rotation silvicultural systems.

Against this background, it would be easy to claim that wilderness is an irrelevant concept in the management of British woodlands. Despite this, wilderness ideals have been a factor in forest planning and management. The prolonged antipathy to upland afforestation with conifers and large-scale clear felling may have been couched in scientific terms, but it was substantially motivated by a feeling that the rectilinearity of forests in an apparently wild environment violated wilderness values. More positively, the currently increasing interest in more discrete and visually harmonious forms of forestry must be partly driven by a desire for more natural environments.

DEFINITION

'*Wilderness*' is taken to mean landscapes in which human influence is – or appears to be – absent or minimal. As a concept it is closely related to '*naturalness*', a concept that is widely used but notoriously difficult to define and delimit. Attitudes to wilderness have been ambivalent: like 'natural' conditions, wilderness has been seen by some people as a threat or at least an undesirable condition, but others have regarded it as interesting, beneficial, reassuring and uplifting.

Two kinds of wilderness are worth recognising:

1. **Original-natural forests**. These are the forests that covered the land before people had much impact. Their condition has been of great interest to scientific ecologists, but they have been largely irrelevant to the general public. If a non-specialist thinks about them at all, he or she probably envisages original forests as evil, disorientating places, populated by dangerous beasts, of which we are well rid.

2. **Minimum intervention stands**. These are stands of any size which are – by design or neglect - 'unmanaged'. Unlike original-natural forests, they exist now, and they are dominated by either native or introduced trees, or mixtures of both. The general public appreciates them as refreshing antidotes to the regularity and intensity of urban living and intensive agriculture. They are also of interest to scientists as baselines or 'controls' for comparison with managed land.

The two kinds of wilderness are linked by the possible survival of elements of original-natural forests in the modern landscape, and by attempts to recreate original-natural forests in reserves.

ORIGINAL-NATURAL WOODLAND

Elements of original-natural woodland survive in the modern landscape in several overlapping forms:

- **Urwälder**. Supposedly virgin forest remnants in Continental Europe.

- **Old-growth**. Stands in North America that have remained virtually untouched since before European settlement.

- **Ancient or primary woods**. Remnants of the original forest cover that have remained in existence continuously since the time when original-natural forests dominated the landscape. Most of these have been utilised for millennia, but mixtures of original-native tree species have survived.

- **Native woods maintained by disturbance**. These woodland types are naturally maintained by episodes of severe disturbance, notably boreal and floodplain types. Continuity of existence on or near the present site is a less important determinant of current characteristics.

All these types have been influenced by people. Even the supposed '*virgin*' forests on continental Europe and the old-growth of North America have all in practice been directly impacted by traditional land managers and wide-scale environmental changes. Nevertheless, all incorporate elements that have been inherited from primitive conditions, such as the complement and distribution of tree and shrub species, mature timber habitats, species with a limited colonising ability, and soils, drainage patterns and land forms that have not been altered by farming and other non-forest land uses. These elements can collectively be regarded as '*inherited-natural*', which recognises both that they have probably been modified to some extent by people, yet they have a direct link to original-natural conditions.

These near-natural and irreplaceable remnants are now highly valued for biodiversity, scientific studies and historical interest. Policies are now in place to retain all or most examples. However, the practical expression of '*wilderness*' is limited to those that are retained as minimum intervention reserves, which, in the absence of major disturbances will probably take the form of high forest stands with a complex patchy structure, large trees, and substantial amounts of deadwood. The objectives of these reserves are primarily scientific, but they will certainly be experienced as tracts of '*wilderness*' by any visitor. A recent report has suggested that in the UK a well-distributed set of fifty to sixty such reserves should be recognised as '*research natural areas*', each one covering at least 30ha with additional buffer zones.

Recently, the character of original-natural forest has become a matter of debate. Most ecologists have assumed that original-natural woodland generally took the form of high forest, but Vera (2000) has argued that large herbivores would have had a substantial impact, and that original-natural forest took the form of wood-pasture. The debate is still unresolved, but the practical implications of accepting the wood-pasture hypothesis seem limited. There would, however, be much interest in establishing large forest reserves with unregulated large herbivore populations, as proposed by Whitbread & Jenman (1995).

DISCRETELY MANAGED FORESTS

The second kind of wilderness is more directly relevant to people in general, rather than scientists in particular, and it has more impact on forest management. It is not a '*pure*' wilderness, but takes the form of '*relative wilderness*' or an illusion of wildness. As such it is part of a wider expression of wildness embodied in moorlands, mountains, lowland heaths and undeveloped coastlines. Here, people can experience landscapes that they perceive as natural, and thereby derive psychological benefits.

The practical expression of this form of wilderness on forest management rarely requires non-intervention, but is best expressed as '*true art conceals art*'. Forests are managed, but discretely in ways that are less immediately obvious to a general visitor than more intensive forms of forestry. The characteristics of this forestry include several or all of the following features:

- Large forests, where internal forest landscapes are dominant and landscapes outside the forest are less obtrusive. [But, small woods can contribute.]

- Long-rotation, high forest silvicultural systems, especially those that embody continuous cover principles. These include classical selection and group-selection systems.

- Native trees are prominent, but not necessarily dominant.

- Stands generally comprise irregular mixtures of tree species.

- Snags and other forms of coarse woody debris are prominent. Some fallen trees retained as they fall, dead or alive.

- Large trees.

- Natural regeneration, i.e., predominantly from seedlings or stump regrowth. Any planting is irregular and patchy.

- Any felling coupes are irregularly shaped and harmonise with land forms.

- Open spaces are present, irregularly shaped, and largely occupying the wet ground and outcrops where they would occur naturally.

- Pasturage is incorporated. This is not just recognition of the points made by Vera (2000), but a means of maintaining open spaces and irregularity irrespective of the validity of his arguments.

- Allowing natural tree lines to develop in upland districts.

Forest management increasingly incorporates these features, and to that extent is increasingly providing the benefits of a wilderness experience. They can be developed in both predominantly native woods and extensive upland conifer plantation forests. Mature retentions are now a standard feature of large forests, and the principles of design have long included shaping forestry operations to the natural land forms. In the Highlands, Forest Enterprise is restoring very large native forests as relative wildernesses, though they do not use this term. A recent report has explored the feasibility of generating '*new wildwoods*' of mainly native trees, especially in the uplands. At Carrifran, Glen Finglas and elsewhere such projects are already under way.

FOREST HABITAT NETWORKS

Providing a wilderness experience is clearly one role of forest and woodland management, though it is rarely couched in those terms. Equally, much of the objection to upland plantation forestry from the 1930s to the 1980s was probably due to infringements of wilderness, through clear-felling mature native stands, straight boundaries, rectilinear planting and felling patterns, 'serried' ranks of planted conifers, and the general elimination of natural habitat variety within plantations.

Even so, *'wilderness'* remains a somewhat nebulous idea that does not provide a firm basis for practical forest design and management. It may be better to base the development of forest structures and patterns on the concept of the Forest Habitat Network (FHN), which can incorporate the full range of forestry objectives and can yield precise specifications. Within a FHN there should be Core Forest Areas, where the wilderness experience would be most developed.

COMPARISON WITH NORTH AMERICA AND CONTINENTAL EUROPE

How do these ideas translate to other parts of the North Temperate Zone? The principal difference is that much of North America and Continental Europe has far more woodland, much larger woods, and in some regions woodland forms the matrix land use. Landscapes of unbroken, lightly-managed, native woodland can be seen in New Jersey from points within sight of downtown New York. Thus, people here live in or close to a near-approach to wilderness. Moreover, wilderness is largely a matter of forest landscapes, not moorland and coast – the Appalachian Trail runs within woodland, and is rarely a place for distant views. Furthermore, the forests are populated by large and sometimes fierce mammals that have been lost from Britain. In short, a high degree of wilderness is just down the road, and the wilderness experience sometimes comes to the kitchen door and turns over one's trashcan.

The effects of these differences on management are considerable. Very large tracts are set aside as national parks and equivalent large reserves in which non-intervention management is the norm. In the eastern USA, a remarkably high proportion of undesignated woodland is allowed to grow naturally, though there are few inhibitions about management or building homes within woodland. Generalising wildly, with so much more forest, it is possible to have wilderness experiences without apparently inhibiting forest management for timber and other objectives.

CONCLUSION

In the UK, *'wilderness'* is associated more with moorlands, mountains and coastlines, where the absence of human influence is more apparent than real. It is a factor in UK forestry, but mainly in the manner of the pastel-artist's foundation colour, which is not seen on the surface, but imbues the surface colours with a strength and resonance that it would not otherwise possess. Absolute wilderness is unobtainable, but relative wilderness can be increased – *'wilder'*, rather than *'wild'*. Forest design and silvicultural treatments must be developed on the basis of more precise criteria.

THE DYNAMIC INFLUENCE OF HISTORY AND ECOLOGY ON THE RESTORATION OF A MAJOR URBAN HEATHLAND AT WHARNCLIFFE, SOUTH YORKSHIRE

Ian D. Rotherham, John C. Rose, and Chris Percy
Sheffield Hallam University

ABSTRACT

Wharncliffe Heath and Crags is in part a recently established, major urban nature reserve in South Yorkshire, England. This site is located on the most easterly of the Peak District Edges, though just outside the Peak District National Park. It was in part for several years a *Yorkshire Wildlife Trust Nature Reserve* managed by the *Sheffield Wildlife Action Partnership (SWAP)* on land owned by the *Forestry Commission*. The site incorporates a *Geological Site of Special Scientific Interest*, *Scheduled Ancient Monuments*, an early Medieval Deer Park, and ancient woodlands. These are all surrounded by and overlooking contemporary housing expansion, road and rail networks, and a mixture of heavy industry and major industrial dereliction. The historic Wharncliffe Chase is still privately owned and surrounding woodland blocks are owned either by Sheffield City Council or by private forestry interests. In recent years (early 2000s) the Yorkshire Wildlife Trust interest lapsed and the nature reserve is now managed by an independent trust.

The history of utilisation and subsequent abandonment, the impacts of industry and urbanisation, and now management as a wildlife site, are all addressed. The contribution of the site to regional biodiversity, being a vital stronghold for locally rare species such as nightjar, red deer, green tiger beetle, adder and grass snake, is discussed, and the dilemmas for local naturalists are noted. In particular, the desire to keep the rare and vulnerable species secret, but in doing so to abandon hope of restoration and management, is noted as a serious constraint and potential threat.

The importance of these species, and of local community support in helping to secure vital grant aid, and a balance of appropriate management and low-key access and promotion, is addressed.

INTRODUCTION

The scale of destruction, abandonment and resulting fragmentation of lowland heaths in the UK is generally recognised (e.g. Gimingham, 1972; Webb, 1986), although this is mostly in relation to the better known, and usually southern, lowland heaths (particularly in Dorset, Hampshire and East Anglia). There has been less attention paid to the often smaller, highly-fragmented and isolated, lowland heaths and low-lying heather moorlands of the midlands and northern England (Rotherham, 1995 and 1996). There are exceptions to this trend which have been highlighted in recent years. National concern over the loss or damage to much of Thorne Moors and Hatfield Chase in South Yorkshire (Caufield, 1991), the long-standing interest of the Yorkshire Wildlife Trust in Askham Bog near York (Fitter and Smith, 1979), and work by Glasson (1987) on the Nottinghamshire heaths, have all helped to raise levels of awareness. Recognition of the regional importance of heathlands led to the publication of the '*Nottinghamshire Heathland Strategy*' (Anon., undated) and policies aimed at conserving relict heathland areas, by Sheffield City Council (Bownes *et al.*,1991) in the early 1990s.

The status of relict heaths and low-lying moorlands in the Sheffield and South Yorkshire region were described by Rotherham (1996 and 1998). The dramatic scale of habitat destruction and degradation over recent centuries has been noted, along with the reasons for loss. The ecological consequences of fragmentation and isolation have been considered, and the former cultural significance of the heaths, moors, and commons highlighted.

The long-term future of heathland environments in the region was discussed, with reference to conservation strategies and issues such as community involvement, funding and environmental benefits. The probable outcomes of continuing decline were considered in the light of recent trends of loss, isolation and extinction. The long-term implications of the inevitable change from sustainable use of this landscape resource by local communities, for fuel, building materials and food, were also discussed.

The arguments relating to the above were supported by case studies demonstrating the potential for site restoration, and where appropriate, habitat re-construction. This identified Wharncliffe Heath and Chase as significant opportunities in this respect.

THE IMPLICATIONS OF SITE FRAGMENTATION AND LOSS, FOR NATURE CONSERVATION AND BIODIVERSITY

Changes in the landscape of this region have been described by Scurfield (e.g.1986), Jones (1989) and Bownes *et al.* (1991). These accounts cover the period from *c.*1500 to *c.*1990, but are not specific in their reference to heaths, moors and commons. The massive scale of change and loss of formerly extensive high-quality semi-natural environments is now very clear. Accounts of the flora of the Sheffield region, particularly the records of Jonathan Salt from the late 1700s, lend credence to this catastrophic change. The loss of Crookesmoor, now in the heart of Sheffield, can be associated with a severe contraction in range of moorland plants, including the regionally rare ivy-leaved bellflower

(*Wahlenbergia hederacea*). This was recorded by Salt in the 1790s around three kilometres west of Sheffield City Centre; by Lees in 1888 around twelve kilometres west on the edge of the Peak District; and now around eighteen kilometres west on Derwent Edge, in the heart of the Peak District National Park.

Some ornithological accounts also indicate the potential scale of change. Blunt (1981) for example, described the former status of red grouse (*Lagopus lagopus*) as both a winter visitor and breeding bird in the lowlands of South Yorkshire, Derbyshire and North Nottinghamshire, during the 1800s until the early 1900s.

The decline of relatively common heathland and moorland species can be easily deduced from an inspection of maps showing the contraction with time, of key habitat-types. However, for less common species, there is little documentary evidence to go on. Some conclusions can be drawn from the present-day, relict distributions of species where they arrive in now fragmented areas of suitable habitat. Emperor moth (*Saturnia pavonia*) and ling pug (*Eupithecia goossensiata*), for example occur on outlying sites such as Wickfield Heath. Common lizard (*Lacerta vivipara*) and perhaps adder (*Vipera berus*) also occur in now widely scattered and isolated, lowland situations.

Reptiles, birds and invertebrates have been identified as key groups to evaluate; and for the invertebrates in particular, much more detailed work will be required before a definitive conclusion can be drawn. However, it is clear that some of the typical moorland/heathland specialists such as green tiger beetle (*Cicindela campestris*), green hairstreak butterfly (*Calliophrys rubi*) and emperor moth (*S. pavonia*) are mobile, and do occur on the larger heathland fragments (e.g. Wharncliffe Heath and Wickfield Heath) but seem to be absent from the smaller sites.

More recent work suggests that whilst estimates of these impacts first presented in 1996 (Rotherham, 1996) may fairly represent the implications for moorland and heathland specialist plants and animals, they grossly under-estimated the overall scale of loss. The effects of these losses on the biodiversity resource generally have undoubtedly been catastrophic. Traditionally managed heaths, moors, commons and bogs typically provide excellent habitat for a whole range of fauna and flora, and usually have feature such as ponds, pools, marshes, woods *etc*. in intimate association with them. The overall change related to enclosure and 'cultural severance' is therefore massive. These are the subject of on-going research.

PAST TRENDS

Changes in land-use have led to a massive loss of heathland and low-lying moor, in areas such as South Yorkshire and North Derbyshire, particularly from around 1600 A.D. to the present day. The most catastrophic losses probably occurred during the sixteenth, seventeenth and eighteenth centuries, associated with Parliamentary and private 'enclosures' of heath, moor, common and 'waste'. The resulting landscape has heather moorland restricted largely to the uplands north-west of Sheffield, in the Peak District National Park. The remaining lowland sites in the east are generally small and highly fragmentary.

Environmental loss on this scale has led to the extinction of a number of specialist species, and severely diminished occurrence of others. Whilst this is often poorly documented, evidence is accumulating to support this conclusion.

THE ENVIRONMENTAL CONSEQUENCES OF THE CHANGES

There are serious and long-term implications of the cultural severance of these areas (described by Rotherham, 1999), from their subsistence exploitation over innumerable centuries. Whilst some of these, such as reinstatement of grazing for example, are being addressed by site managers, others are intractable. The long-term exploitation for fuel in particular must be seen as fundamental in maintaining low-nutrient status; essential for many of the specialist species. Abandonment of this use has allowed a gradual but perhaps irreversible move towards eutrophication that will have profound implications in the long-term.

THE WHARNCLIFFE CASE STUDY SITE

The Wharncliffe area has long been known as one of the finest wildlife sites in the Sheffield district. The area is in the core zone of the *South Yorkshire Forest*. The Forest Team commissioned a comprehensive biological survey in 1993 to be carried out by the *Sheffield City Ecology Unit*; this was the first comprehensive ecological assessment of the complex. Within the Forest Core Area are Wharncliffe Wood, Wharncliffe Chase and Heath, Greno Wood, Hall Wood, Prior Royd Wood, Wheata Wood and Birkin Royd Wood. The present account considers only the first three. The area has particular significance as the most easterly of the Peak District edges and moorlands. Although it includes a large area of 'intermediate-level' moorland, much of this has the character of lowland heath, and was accepted as such in the proposals for Countryside Stewardship funding to the then Countryside Commission. This plant community and its environment or habitat-type is rare in the Sheffield area today. Unmanaged, much of the interest was under serious and imminent threat.

INTRODUCTION TO THE STUDY AREA

The *Greno-Wharncliffe Core Area* is a mosaic of deciduous, semi-natural and plantation, woodland, heathland and acid grassland. The area is floristically relatively impoverished, due to a mix of inherent environmental character relating to acidic substrates and exposed conditions, to gross levels of air pollution in the recent past, and to both intensive forestry and patchily intensive grazing. Associated with both, the latter has been extensive land drainage. However, in most of the woods there remain patches of much richer woodland flora; perhaps indicative of how things once were. These are usually along streams and woodland edges. In contrast to the relative poverty of the flora, the faunal interest of the complex is considerable. Several bird species are at the edge of their ranges and Wharncliffe Heath is one of the few remaining intermediate moorland habitat-types in the region, supporting the area's largest breeding population of nightjar (*Caprimulgus europaeus*). There are also locally and regionally significant breeding populations of reptiles and amphibians. Wharncliffe Woods have been extensively researched for their invertebrate fauna and are notable a diversity of insect species, in particular the Coleoptera (beetles) and Syrphidae (hoverflies). Wharncliffe Wood and Heath, together with the Greno Wood area, are listed as Grade B (regionally significant) on the *English Nature Invertebrate Site Register*. The area is also of special archaeological and geological significance; Wharncliffe Crags being designated an *SSSI (Site of Special Scientific Interest)* and with *RIGS (Regionally Important Geological Sites)* as well. Part of the site is a Scheduled Ancient Monument, and a much wider area is now recognised as being of great conservation interest for its archaeology.

The main land tenure of the case study site is shared between two land owners. Wharncliffe Chase, together with some adjacent farmland and woodland, is owned and managed by Wharncliffe Estates Ltd., whilst Wharncliffe Wood and Wharncliffe Heath are owned by the Forestry Commission and managed by Forest Enterprise.

PAST AND PRESENT LAND USE

Evidence of early human activity in the area dates back to around 7,500 B.C. Close to the confluence of the Don and Little Don rivers at Deepcar, is a nationally important Mesolithic site, probably used as a summer camp by hunters following seasonal animal migrations to the uplands of the Pennines. The Wharncliffe area was intensively used during the Romano-British period, and settlements from this time have been excavated at Wheata Wood, Greno Wood, Hannah Moor, Gosling Moor, Stockthorn, and at Whitley 'Church'. The remains of buildings and field boundaries have been identified under what is now the Wharncliffe Chase boundary.

The Crags were quarried extensively during this period for quern-stones (hand mills for grinding grain) which, it is thought, gave rise to the original name '*Quern Cliff*'. The disc-shaped base stones and beehive-shaped rotating stones can still be found at the base of the crag, mostly as unfinished artefacts. During the early medieval period the first of a series of enclosures of the

Chase took place. These were carried out between the early thirteenth and late sixteenth centuries and much of the area was subsequently developed as a '*deer park*'. The remains of two villages, the inhabitants of which were evicted during the enclosures, can still be found within the present Chase boundary. There is much evidence of past industrial use, particularly within Wharncliffe Wood, the most notable being mining. The local coals and their associated gannister and fire-clay have been extensively worked and several old drift mines and adits are in evidence on the talus slope below Wharncliffe Crags. Grenoside sandstone was quarried throughout Greno Wood and the eastern Chase, and was renowned as a high quality building stone.

Organised exploitation of the woodland resource has probably been ongoing for at least 600 years. Management probably took the form of '*coppice-with-standards*' until the nineteenth century when the planting of conifers such as Scots pine and larch was carried out. By the early part of this century traditional woodland management had all but ceased. There is some evidence that coppicing continued in parts of Birkin Wood until more recently, with derelict hazel stools found along the north-eastern boundary. Both landscape and vegetation have been considerably modified during the twentieth century. Large areas of Wharncliffe Wood were felled during World War One, during the General Strike in 1926, and to a lesser extent during World War Two (Grenoside Conservation Society, 1974). Further destruction of the woods took place during the period up to 1954 when woodland adjacent to the railway was destroyed in a series of severe fires caused by the sparks from passing steam trains (A. Brackenbury pers. comm.).

Since this time, the dominant land use has been commercial forestry, with blanket afforestation of the southern section of Wharncliffe Woods and much of Greno Wood. This has reduced what was described in 1903 by W. G. Smith (former President of the British Ecological Society) as "*probably one of the finest oak woods in the country*" to a much simplified community. However, due to local pressure, the planting of Wharncliffe was quite varied (by the Forestry Commission standards at that time) and landscape considerations were taken into account. Important in this was the fact that the Upper Don Valley and Wharncliffe in particular, were well known tourism destinations and hence very much in the public eye.

More recently, the area has experienced intensive and largely unplanned recreational use. This includes informal activities such as walking and jogging, but also more intensive and organised pastimes such as mountain biking, orienteering, horse riding, clay pigeon shooting and fox hunting. Rock climbing is carried out on Wharncliffe Crags, a site many local climbers consider to have been the birth-place of the sport in the Peak District. All of these activities have the potential for causing serious environmental damage.

HABITAT-TYPES

Woodland is the most extensive habitat-type, with the largest continuous block of woodland in the South Yorkshire Community Forest area. Up to the early 1950's, all that remained of the ancient Wharncliffe Wood was mostly open birch, willow and bracken scrub, with older areas of mature birch (*Betula* sp.) and oak (*Quercus* sp.), and occasional yew (*Taxus baccata*), sweet chestnut (*Castanea sativa*) and sycamore (*Acer pseudoplatanus*). An alder-dominated canopy persisted alongside springs and wet-flushes (A. Brackenbury, pers. comm.). Since this period, approximately half of the total area of Wharncliffe Wood has been planted with conifers and as a result much of the semi-natural deciduous woodland has been lost. The ancient woodland is now almost entirely restricted to small pockets along steep stream-sides in the southern half of the wood. The best remaining areas can be found as narrow strips alongside the stream dividing Wharncliffe Wood and Birkin Royd, alongside Stead Spring and at the lower end of the valley known as Waterfall Clough. In these areas the canopy is dominated by oak and birch with rowan (*Sorbus aucuparia*) on the drier slopes, and by alder and hazel (*Corylus avellana*) in damper areas beside stream-sides. The field layer is occasionally very rich, especially in damp areas where species such as yellow archangel (*Lamiastrum galeobdolon*) and wood sorrel (*Oxalis acetosella*) may occur in great profusion together with Sphagnum mosses and mats of other bryophytes. Other species typical of these relict habitats include wood sage (*Teucrium scorodonia*), dog's mercury (*Mercurialis perennis*), great wood-rush (*Luzula sylvatica*) and grasses such as wood millet (*Milium effusum*) and wood melick (*Melica uniflora*). Some of the plantations have retained a relict field-layer, with species including yellow archangel, bluebell (*Hyacinthoides non-scripta*), wood sorrel, and herb robert (*Geranium robertianum*). Areas of wind-throw, or where felling has taken place and replanting has not been carried out, birch and oak, have begun to colonise with an understorey of dense bracken (*Pteridium aquilinum*). Where there is a high water-table the ground flora may be quite diverse and include mosses such as *Sphagnum* spp. and several species of rush (*Juncus* spp.).

Secondary, deciduous woodland runs almost the entire length of Wharncliffe Wood and is the main canopy type below Wharncliffe Crags. This canopy is ecologically rather uniform with large areas dominated by birch with occasional oak, sycamore and holly (*Ilex aquilinum*). The understorey is sparse to absent except in areas of wind-throw where seedlings and saplings of oak and birch may be present. The field layer is typically species poor and consists mostly of wavy hair-grass (*Deschampsia flexuosa*) or creeping soft grass (*Holcus mollis*) with occasional herb species such as wood sage and climbers such as honeysuckle (*Lonicera periclymenum*). Ericaceous shrubs such as heather (*Calluna vulgaris*) and Bilberry (*Vaccinium myrtillus*) are also present.

Bracken and bramble (*Rubus fruticosus* agg.) are locally dominant. Scattered throughout these birch-dominated areas are patches of older, probably planted, deciduous trees such as sycamore, beech (*Fagus sylvatica*) and sweet chestnut (*Castanea sativa*), as well as remnants of an even older, more diverse, stunted oak / birch / rowan woodland. In these latter areas the canopy rarely attains more than seven metres in height and is either dominated by sessile oak (*Quercus petraea*) or an oak / birch mix, with scattered rowan. The *Grade A Local Red Data Book* species, climbing corydalis (*Corydalis claviculata*) is present.

Throughout the wood, ride margins have developed into an important network of wildlife habitats. Some have survived as open heather / bilberry heath, whilst others have ditches supporting marsh willowherb (*Epilobium palustre*), yellow pimpernel (*Lysimachia nemorum*), skullcap (*Scutellaria galericulata*), square-stalked St. John's-wort (*Hypericum tetrapterum*). lesser spearwort (*Ranunculus flammula*) and a variety of rushes. Bracken dominates many drier stretches but many other species are also frequent. These include perforate and slender St. John's-wort (*H. perforatum* and *H. pulchrum*), common figwort (*Scrophularia nodosa*), foxglove (*Digitalis purpurea*), tormentil (*Potentilla erecta*), and bird's foot trefoil (*Lotus comiculatus*). These open ride sides support a diversity of insect species, provide ecological links between larger open areas and add to the diversity of environments and potential habitats.

Vegetation on Wharncliffe Chase is a mosaic of acid grassland and encroaching bracken in drier areas, with rush and sedge dominated communities in damp hollows and on the margins of ponds. The grassland is locally dominated by sheep's fescue (*Festuca ovina*), common bent (*Agrostis capillaris*), sweet vernal grass (*Anthoxanthum odoratum*) and wavy hair-grass. Mat grass (*Nardus stricta*) communities are extensive and characteristically species-poor; probably a result of intensive grazing. Other species include herbs such as tormentil and heath bedstraw (*Galium saxatile*) and rushes such as compact rush (*Juncus conglomeratus*), heath rush (*J. squarrosus*) and soft rush (*J. effusus*). Comparison of aerial photographs from 1989 and field survey results showed bracken to have spread considerably during the early 1990s; covering over half the total area of the Chase.

A number of old stock ponds are present on the Chase, together with several larger wet areas where stream drainage has been impeded. These are the richest communities on the Chase and contain species of damp, saturated and open water conditions such as tufted hair-grass (*Deschampsia cespitosa*), common cotton-grass (*Eriophorum angustifolium*), soft and compact rush, marsh bedstraw, marsh willowherb, skullcap, marsh pennywort (*Hydrocotyle vulgaris*) and lesser spearwort. Several areas of previously open water are now being invaded by mosses. Creeping soft-grass is usually dominant together with wood millet, ivy (*Hedera helix*), yellow archangel and bluebell. Other species are locally abundant and include wood melick, dog's mercury, wood sorrel, common dog violet, greater stitchwort, ground ivy (*Glechoma hederacea*), lesser celandine (*Ranunculus ficaria*), wood sage, broad buckler-fern (*Dryopteris dilatata*) and male fern (*D. filix-mas*), with sweet woodruff (*Galium odoratum*), lords-and-ladies (*Arum maculatum*), and climbing corydalis.

The oak canopy is more diverse and better structured although it has a more species-poor field layer of wavy hair-grass, creeping soft-grass, bracken and bramble. The richest ground flora occurs close to the stream and includes opposite-leaved golden saxifrage (*Chrysosplenium oppositifolium*), wood anemone (*Anemone nemorosa*), yellow pimpernel, marsh bedstraw (*Galium palustre*), bog stitchwort (*Stellaria uliginosa*), wood speedwell (*Veronica montana*), angelica (*Angelica sylvestris*), common valerian, common figwort, red campion (*Silene dioica*), cow parsley (*Anthriscus sylvestris*), hedge woundwort (*Stachys sylvatica*) and marsh violet (*Viola palustris*). The precipitous slopes support good populations of lady fern (*Athyrium felis-femina*), hard fern (*Blechnum spicant*) and greater wood-rush.

Wharncliffe Heath is an area of heather-dominated dry heath, the main lying immediately east of the northern end of Wharncliffe Crags. The heath reaches its widest point (some 250 metres) north of the Chase and ultimately grades into scrub woodland. Much of the heath is dominated by heather, bracken and birch scrub. Unlike the generally wetter moorlands in the Peak District, the site is situated at relatively low altitude (around 500 metres) on a leached mineral soil and is floristically rather poor. Apart from heather, few of the ericoid species associated with peat or damper soils are present, although bilberry is occasional, together with broom (*Cytisus scoparius*) and gorse (*Ulex europaeus*). Crowberry (*Empetrum nigrum*) occurs as a single patch at the northern end of the site. The restricted diversity is probably related to the dry conditions, and generally free-draining nature of the area, influenced perhaps by management history. Even localised wet areas are generally species-poor and dominated by species such as tufted hair-grass, purple moor-grass (*Molinia caerulea*) and rushes.

FAUNA

The wide range of habitat-types found at the site supports a rich and diverse fauna including a number of locally and nationally endangered species. Wharncliffe Wood provides the principle habitat for a herd of red deer (*Cervus elaphus*), a *Grade A Local Red Data Book* species. There are almost certainly the descendants of the original herd that existed on Wharncliffe Chase. The herd is known to range widely throughout the area, including Bitholmes Wood and the Ewden Valley, west as far as the eastern moorland fringe of the Peak District National Park (see McCarthy and Rotherham, 1994). Another Grade A Local Red Data Book species, roe deer (*Capreolus capreolus*) is also present. There are several active setts of badger (*Meles meles*) within Wharncliffe Wood, including one located under a rock outcrop in an old gannister working. This sett is long-established and remains very active as evidenced by the large number of well-worn paths radiating through the surrounding area. Red squirrel (*Sciurus vulgaris*) for which the last sighting was in 1987, is now extinct here.

The ornithological interest on the site is very high, with a wide variety of woodland and moorland species present, including several with *Red Data Book* status. Of these the most noteworthy is nightjar, a *National Grade A Red Data Book* species for which Wharncliffe is the most important breeding site in the Sheffield area. During the post-1950s period, the breeding range of nightjar contracted significantly (Burgess *et al.*, 1990). This further highlighted the importance of the area when even then it retained its population. Wharncliffe Heath and adjacent areas have been surveyed regularly since the 1970's by the Sheffield Bird Study Group and the British Trust for Ornithology. The results of surveys indicate a breeding population of around six pairs. During the 1940s and 1950s, nightjar was a common nesting species at Wharncliffe, utilising both the high and low sections of Wharncliffe Wood, wherever open ground was present (A. Brackenbury pers. comm.).

Nightjar declined as the woodland canopy closed and with conifer planting; although young plantations can be good habitat. It is now confirmed as breeding only on the crag-top environment of Wharncliffe Heath. Other breeding bird species of note include spotted flycatcher (*Muscicapa striata*) and curlew (*Numenius arquata*). For the latter Wharncliffe Chase is one of the most easterly breeding sites in the region. Recently recorded breeding species include woodcock (*Scolopax rusticola*), sparrowhawk (*Accipiter nisus*), cuckoo (*Cuculus canorus*), great spotted and green woodpeckers (*Dendrocopus major* and *Picus viridis*), tree pipit (*Anthus trivialis*), whitethroat (*Sylvia communis*), garden warbler (*S. borin*), tawny owl (*Strix aluco*), little owl (*Athene noctua*), siskin (*Carduelis pinus*), nuthatch (*Sitta europaea*), and barn owl (*Tyto alba*).

Six species of reptile and amphibian are present including common lizard (*Lacerta vivipara*), grass snake (*Natrix natrix*) and adder (*Vipera beris*). The latter is now locally rare as a result of habitat loss and is a *Grade A Local Red Data Book* species. Populations have recently been reported at Wharncliffe Reservoir, and along the disused railway track to the west of Wharncliffe Crags. Palmate newt (*Triturus helveticus*) is present in the large pond to the north-east of the Heath; by far the largest colony in South Yorkshire or North Derbyshire.

Wharncliffe Woods have been well researched for their invertebrate fauna, with systematic records dating back to the late 1800's. The site is on the *English Nature Invertebrate Site Register* and is nationally known for its diversity of insect species.

SITE RESTORATION AND CONSERVATION

Establishing the Heath as a nature reserve was perhaps the most significant achievement of the current initiative. Here the desired management objectives were pretty easy to agree but more difficult to achieve. A programme of controlled burning, of birch cutting and more recently of grazing with rare breeds livestock is pulling the site back in the right direction to at least maintain the area as heathland. There have been some difficulties and compromises. This is a sensitive area for wildlife, recreation, scientific geological interest and archaeology. The work to promote nature conservation effectively re-kindled interest in the site's archaeology, leading to particularly significant outcomes. Recent surveys on behalf of English Heritage have identified the area as the most important Romano-British quern factory in the UK and possibly in Europe. This has serious implications for some of the proposed nature conservation management, and in fact on a conservation scale the archaeology is of greater significance than the ecology alone.

There is also a potential conflict between desires to improve access and to maintain the natural fabric and allow experience of that. So when a conservation implementation officer took a team out to chip off the rough boulders from the main footpath to the Crags, in order to improve access, the damage to the geological SSSI was inexcusable. The idea was sound but totally outside the management plan brief, and a damaging act to the SSSI; a well-meaning but potentially damaging action on a complex and vulnerable site.

The proposals for the Chase also highlight the need for a careful and holistic approach to historic sites even when they appear to be in desperate need of management. The Chase was seen as a huge opportunity to re-establish heathland close to the Crags and the Heath itself. Grant aid in the form of *Countryside Stewardship* was available to both areas, and has underpinned much of the work. On the Chase, grant was taken up to decrease the levels of grazing stock and hopefully tackle the expansion of bracken. However, there was also the chance to re-establish heather in a more radical approach to the site. Site survey indicated a total absence of heather on the Chase but expanding bracken and poor acidic grassland. This therefore seemed an ideal opportunity to intervene and to either re-seed heather or even encourage natural regeneration. After all it was felt that heather had been present not that long ago. The Chase has a number of stone and sod revetted mounds, described on the Ordnance Survey maps as 'butts', and it was well-known that the Earls of Wharncliffe had used the site for shooting. The conclusion was that these were indeed shooting butts for grouse shoots, and therefore the site must have be heath or moorland within the last 100-150 years. Unfortunately, this interpretation was completely wrong. Samples of soil taken to examine dormant seed banks produced no heather at all. This seemed perplexing, but perhaps the heather was lost too long ago. However, in discussion with both Melvyn Jones and Albert Henderson, a totally different conclusion was arrived at, and therefore alternative recommendation for the site. The '*butts*' are not grouse butts at all, but are medieval pillow mounds for keeping rabbits, and of great historic interest. The use for shooting was for target practice by soldiers from the estate during wartime training and not after grouse at all! It is probably over five hundred years at least since heather formed the dominant community on the Chase, and perhaps not even then.

Quite clearly, restoration of this historically important and complex area to heathland would have been both problematic to achieve also misconceived in conservation terms. The present management will seek to decrease grazing, to allow the Chase to recover any diversity '*naturally*', and perhaps encourage the land-owner to allow some areas to recover from drainage operations that have substantially de-watered the entire site. Heathland restoration has been targeted at the Heath and then at areas of the wood below the main Crags.

Needless to say, further work on the historic landscape of the area is required and is on-going. However, this study does provide an important lesson in terms of the need for effective collaboration. Without a close dialogue between historians, ecologists, archaeologists, and managers, the full interest of this exciting complex would have remained unknown. Furthermore, active conservation management could have proved very damaging to some aspects of the interest.

There is a final issue that arises from the project to date. This concerns public access and site profile for what is a regionally and nationally important site. It is vulnerable and needs careful management and this has a cost. Unfortunately it is not possible to raise funds for work of this sort without promoting the site to a wider public. This raises all sorts of issues in a democracy such as ours. However, the idea of keeping the site 'quiet' simply allowed the ecological successions to proceed in a totally predictable way. The consequences of this are themselves totally predictable and transparent. The desire to protect the site by silence is completely understandable, but also seriously misconceived. The challenge is surely to balance access, education, management and protection; and to pay for it all as well. In recent years this has been achieved by volunteer input, sympathetic support from the Forestry Commission, and grant aid from the then Countryside Commission's *Countryside Stewardship* fund. Surveys were paid for by the South Yorkshire Forest Partnership. Most recently grant aid has been provided by the Heritage Lottery Fund for a heathland conservation project originally promoted by the South Yorkshire Biodiversity Research Group and Sheffield Hallam University.

FUTURE POTENTIAL

Future priorities are the maintenance and conservation of remaining relict moorlands and heathlands. However, interesting secondary heather areas will also be safeguarded where possible, and new sites created when opportunities arise (Bownes et al., 1991). Exciting possibilities identified in the early 1990s, included the restoration of degraded former heather sites such as Wharncliffe Chase (c.3-6 square kilometres), through grant-aid schemes like Countryside Stewardship, and the integration of new heather communities into land-restoration and re-development proposals. Careful design and implementation would produce new, low-cost landscapes which are, low maintenance and of relatively high wildlife value. Where possible, these opportunities will be used to buffer and enhance the relict sites (such as for example Wharncliffe Heath). These heather-dominated communities are attractive, ecologically interesting, popular with the public and usually, very low-cost to establish and maintain. This should make them attractive features for land managers in the future. However, for long term success, the vision needs to be wider and more ambitious. The erosion of this landscape that has occurred increasingly over the last 200 years needs to be addressed and this will mean re-naturing a substantial zone around the core area. Without a long-term and coherent programme of restoration and reversion of recent trends the core areas will remain isolated and at risk from further degradation. Simply protecting and maintaining what we now have will not be enough.

ACKNOWLEDGEMENTS

Thanks are due to the many individuals and organisations who have contributed information. In particular we wish to thank both Chris James and Caroline Boffey for assistance with fieldwork, Andrew McCarthy and Kay Dulieu for their contributions to research and fieldwork, and Joan Butt for the graphics, and Paul Ardron and the late Gordon Scurfield for much-needed inspiration! Mel Jones and Albert Henderson have given helpful advice on the site and its historic interpretation. The Yorkshire Wildlife Trust and SWAP, together with the reserve committee are making it all happen, along with the land-owner (the Forest Enterprise team) and the South Yorkshire Forest Partnership. Many other local people have also helped along the way.

REFERENCES

Anon. (undated) *Nottinghamshire Heathland Strategy*. Nottinghamshire County Council, Nottingham.

Anon. (1974) *Report on the Proposed Country Park study area*. Grenoside Conservation Society, Sheffield.

Anon. (1994) *An Ecological Survey of the Wharncliffe Area*. Sheffield City Ecology Unit, Sheffield.

Blunt, A.G. (1981) The Red Grouse in Lowland Yorkshire, *Magpie*, **2**, 1-2

Bownes, J.S., Riley, T.H., Rotherham, I.D. and Vincent, S.M. (1991) *Sheffield Nature Conservation Strategy*, Sheffield City Council, Sheffield.

Caufield, C. (1991) *Thorne Moors*. The Sumach Press, St. Albans.

Gimingham, C.H. (1972) *Ecology of Heathland*, Chapman and Hall, London.

Glasson, N. (1987) Heathland Loss in Nottinghamshire since 1927, *Landscape Research*, **12(1)**, 13-18.

Jones, M. (1989) *Sheffield's Woodland Heritage*, Green Tree Publications, Rotherham.

McCarthy, A.J. (1996) *Wharncliffe Heath Nature Reserve Management Plan 1996-2001*. Sheffield Centre for Ecology and Environmental Management, Sheffield.

McCarthy, A.J. (1996) *Wharncliffe Chase Conservation Plan 1996-2001*. Sheffield Centre for Ecology and Environmental Management, Sheffield.

McCarthy, A.J. (2000) *Wharncliffe Heath Nature Reserve – A Heathland Management Plan 2000-2003*. Andrew McCarthy Ecology, Sheffield.

McCarthy, A.J., Dulieu, K., Rotherham, I.D. and Milego, C. (1993) The Natural History of the Wharncliffe Area. *Sorby Record*, **30**, 7-19.

McCarthy, A.J. and Rotherham, I.D. (1994) Deer in the Sheffield Region including the Eastern Peak District. *Naturalist*, **119**, 103-110.

Parry, M.L. (1977) *Mapping Moorland Change: A Framework for Land-Use Decisions in the Peak District*, Peak District National Park, Bakewell

Rackham, O. (1986) *The History of the Countryside*. Dent, London.

Rotherham, I.D. (1995) Urban Heathlands - Their Conservation, Restoration and Creation. *Landscape Contamination and Reclamation*, **3(2)**, 99-100

Rotherham, I.D. (1996) *Habitat Fragmentation and Isolation in Relict Urban Heathlands - the ecological consequences and future potential*, Abstract paper in: *The Proceedings of the 28th International Geographical Congress*. August 1996. The Hague, The Netherlands. (unpublished)

Rotherham, I.D., Ardron, P.A. and Gilbert, O.L. (1997) Peat cutters and their Landscapes: fundamental change in a fragile environment. Peatland Ecology and Archaeology: management of a cultural landscape. Landscape Conservation Forum Conference, 29 October 1997, Sheffield. (Unpublished).

Rotherham, I.D. (1999) *Peat cutters and their Landscapes: fundamental change in a fragile environment*. In: Peatland Ecology and Archaeology: management of a cultural landscape. *Landscape Archaeology and Ecology*, **4**, 28-51.

Scurfield, G. and Medley, I.E. (1952) An Historical Account of the Vegetation in the Sheffield District: the vegetation of the Southall Soake in 1637. *Transactions of the Hunter Archaeological Society*, **7**, 63-77.

Scurfield, G. and Medley, I.E. (1957) An Historical Account of the vegetation in the Sheffield District: the Parish of Ecclesfield in 1637. *Transactions of the Hunter Archaeological Society*, **7**, 180-187.

Scurfield, G. (1986) Seventeenth Century Sheffield and Environs. *Yorkshire Archaeological Journal*, **58**, 147-171.

Webb, N. (1986) *Heathlands*. Collins, London.

Ploughing on regardless? The effects of cultivation in the landscape

Organised by the **Landscape Conservation Forum**, the seminar took place on October 29th 2003. It considered the impacts of cultivation on our natural and historic environments, how they have and are being assessed and how damage can be mitigated. It raised issues of the ways in which Environmental Impact Assessment (EIA) can protect uncultivated land from improvement. Speakers and participants included landscape professionals, archaeologists, ecologists, earth scientists, planners, conservationists and workers in education.

Programme

Introduction and Welcome: Ian Rotherham, Sheffield Hallam University, Landscape Conservation Forum.

Morning Session:

Chair: Ken Smith, Peak District National Park Authority

George Lambrick, Council for British Archaeology: *The impacts of cultivation: management of archaeological sites in arable landscapes.*

Martin Harper, Conservation Director, Plantlife International *Farmland flowers: the implications of cultivation.*

Jon Humble, English Heritage: *Pilot projects in the East Midlands and a national campaign: evidence-based approaches in the quest for hearts, minds and money.*

Tim Melling, RSPB: *Upland ploughland – boon or bane for wildlife?*

Afternoon Session:

Chair: Rhodri Thomas, Peak District National Park Authority

John Seymour, NFU: *Farming with Heritage - the practicalities.*

Bob Middleton, Rural Development Service, Defra: *Ploughing, participation and partners - agri-environment schemes and arable archaeology.*

Andrew Adams, Defra: *Uncultivated land and semi-natural areas: agriculture and the EIA regulations.*

Discussion

Ian Rotherham, Chair, Landscape Conservation Forum: *Concluding remarks.*

THE EFFECTS OF PLOUGHING ON ANCIENT TREES
Ted Green

INTRODUCTION

Ploughing can damage trees in two ways:

1. Physical damage to roots and mycorrhizal root associations which affects living systems and also may allow pathogens to attack vulnerable roots; and

2. Cutting off of lower limbs to allow vehicle access. These are often major limbs and the larger the wound the more impact this will have on the tree in the long-term.

EFFECTS ON ROOTS AND ASSOCIATED ORGANISMS

It is believed that the root system of a tree is a very different shape to the above-ground structures as shown in the picture above. Most roots spread out in the top 600 mm of the soil up to 2.5 times the circumference of the canopy. Although roots may retrench as trees age and their canopy reduces it is possible for the root system to become asymmetrical and therefore a precautionary approach should be taken in changing the environment around ancient trees.

Deep ploughing is of greatest concern and can lead to gradual loss of trees in a landscape.

The tree below is host to the Oak Polypore – a scheduled species under the *Wildlife and Countryside Act 1981*, but the host ancient tree is in danger of being lost due to deep ploughing – see the stag headed canopy suddenly reduced by environmental impact.

Best Practice is outlined in the handbook *Veteran Trees – a Guide to Good Management*. A minimum intervention area around each tree of 15 times the diameter of the tree is called for to avoid undue damage to root systems. This is increasingly being accepted in agri-environment schemes.

... and after.

If machines can get close in to trees then there are additional effects of muck spreading which can damage important lichen communities on tree trunks and the application of inorganic fertilisers which damage mycorrhizal fungi.

CUTTING OFF LOWER LIMBS FOR VEHICLE ACCESS

The long-term effects of cutting off lower limbs of trees to allow vehicle access can be seen in these two pictures – before ...

BEST PRACTICE

The Woodland Trust and Ancient Tree Forum believe that the best arboricultural practice should be used if lower limbs need to be reduced to minimise the untimely demise of important trees.

PLOUGHING, PARTICIPATION AND PARTNERS: AGRI-ENVIRONMENT SCHEMES AND ARABLE ARCHAEOLOGY

Bob Middleton
Rural Development Service, Defra

INTRODUCTION

- Sustainable development underpinned by PSA targets.

- Delivery tools:

  - Cross –compliance;

  - Regulation (e.g. EIA);

  - England Rural Development Plan.

AGRI-ENVIRONMENT (AE)

- Countryside Stewardship Scheme (CSS) and Environmentally Sensitive Areas (ESA):

  - ESA: 22 landscape areas designated 1987-1994;

  - CSS: started 1991 outside ESAs;

  - Objectives: wildlife, landscape, access and historic environment;

  - 10-year voluntary agreements with farmers and owners to manage landscape sustainably.

THE AGRI-ENVIRONMENT CONTRIBUTION

Spend (£m)	2002-3	2003-4
ESA	52	53
CSS	53	69
(RES	9.8	21)

- Since 1998 £30m on protection of Historic Environment;

- In 2002 £13m spent on Historic Environment (£8m ESA, £5m CSS);

- By 2001 21,000km boundaries restored; and

- 20-40% RES involve conversion of Traditional Buildings.

CSS spend 02-03 (£m)	6.017
% boundaries	78
% built structures	8
ESA spend 02-03 (£m)	7.679
% boundaries	26
% built structures	51

DESIGNATED SITES ON AE SCHEME HOLDINGS

Scheduled Monuments	25% of no
World Heritage Sites	25% of area
Parks and Gardens	20% of area
Battlefields	10% of area

ARABLE MANAGEMENT

- Vital for some wildlife - birds and rare plants.
- Can weaken landscape character.
- Damages historic environment.

EFFECTS OF ARABLE CULTIVATION ON THE HISTORIC ENVIRONMENT

- Mechanical damage to sites:
  - ploughing; and
  - sub-soiling.
- Damage through works associated with cultivation:
  - levelling;
  - stone removal;
  - drainage; and
  - earthwork removal.

- Change in historic character through field boundary loss and landscape features.
- Isolation of protected sites leading to neglect and loss through scrub encroachment and burrowing animals.

AE ARABLE MANAGEMENT

- Do not increase arable (CC).
- Arable options – over-wintered stubbles, wildflower mixes and conservation headlands for wildlife.
- Grass margins for wildlife and historic environment.
- Reversion to permanent grassland for landscape, wildlife and historic environment.

STONEHENGE / AVEBURY WORLD HERITAGE SITE

- CSS Special Project 2002 to fulfil Management Plan objectives.
- Targeted reversion of arable to permanent pasture.
- 2002 – 129ha
- 2003 – 200ha
- By end 2003 the following reverted:
  - Normanton Down Barrows;
  - North Kite enclosure; and
  - Durrington Down Barrows.
- Increased access and enhance setting for monuments.

COTSWOLDS ESA COBBERLEY

- **Discovered by metal detectorists 2003 following sub-soiling.**

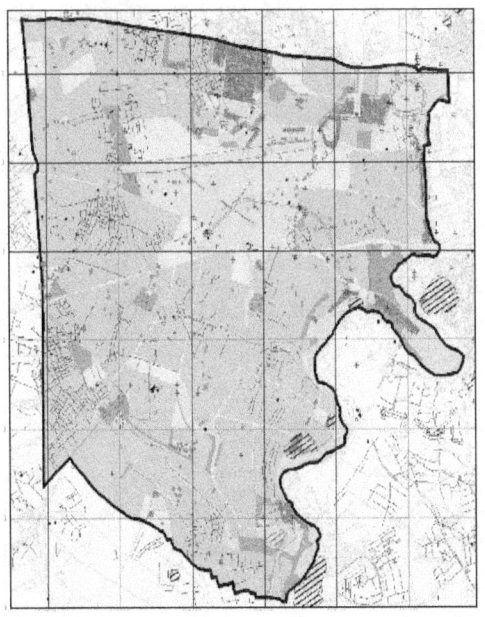

- **Ploughed annually for at least 20 years, sub-soiled every 10 years.**
- **5ha now in arable reversion with cutting regime.**

SOME MAJOR ISSUES

- Range of options for sites under cultivation.
- Take up of arable reversion.
- Historic values of arable.

OPTIONS - Research and Development (R&D)

- Measures to protect sites whilst cultivation continues.
- Accurate site assessment to determine risk.
- Better understanding of effects of cultivation.

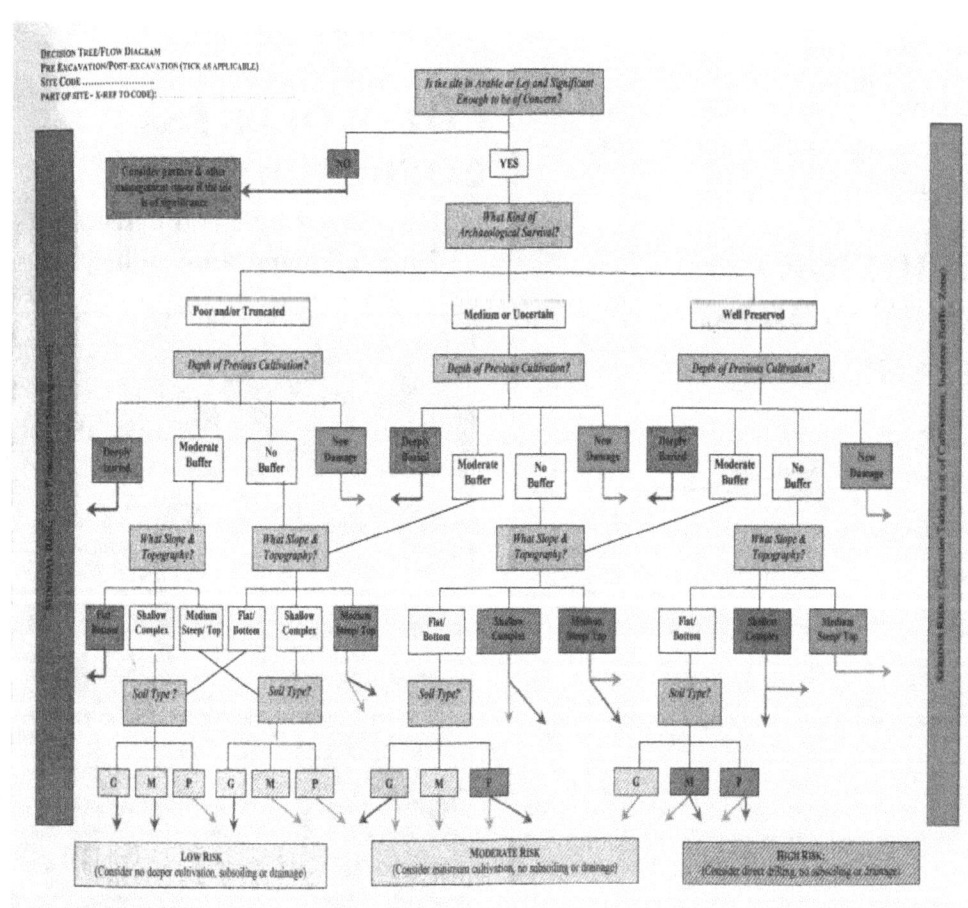

R&D: BD1701

- Identify nation priorities through *National Plough Risk Model*.
- Develop *Site Assessment Model* for assessing sites for action.
- Identify sustainable management options.
- Identify policy options.

TAKE UP OF ARABLE REVERSION

- Payment rates.
- Site management issues:
  - Grazing;
  - Fencing;
  - Water supply; and
  - Access.

AGRI-ENVIRONMENT REVIEW

- Third Consultation.
- Proposed measures to encourage arable management.
- Enhancements to reflect real costs of arable management – in-field and HQL supplements.
- Minimum till options.
- Resource protection options.

HISTORIC VALUES OF ARABLE

- Arable can represent an important continuity of land-use.
- The cycle of arable cultivation has high cultural values and engenders a 'sense of place', e.g. harvest festivals.
- Loss of arable detrimental to landscape character.
- Exmoor:

  1962 – 10% cereals and roots.

  1992 – 2% cereals and roots.

FARMING WITH HERITAGE - THE PRACTICALITIES

John Seymour
Heritage Spokesman, National Farmers' Union

FARMING – THE CONTEXT FOR HERITAGE

The role and functions of farming provide both a context for heritage, and the lineage of farming can in itself be heritage. There are key aspects of farming that relate to this:

- Agriculture is a primary producer.

- Significant force in the rural economy.

- Europe's countryside is a product of farming:

  - Managed landscapes;

  - Dependent wildlife habitats and species;

  - Cultural landscapes – a record of past use and significance; and

  - Provider of recreational and tourist assets.

- Without farming heritage features and cultural landscapes would be lost on a massive scale.

- This provides a context for *'farming with heritage'*.

- But there is one key driver on farming practice and policy and that is funding. In relation to this in recent years there have been major changes in policy, strategy and funding itself.

- CAP reform.

- Market priorities.

- Environmental legislation.

- Other influences include EU Water Framework Directive and soil strategies (particularly in relation to diffuse pollution and soil conservation). There is also specific guidance and legislation acting at a landscape scale. This includes:

  - Heritage legislation; and

  - Countryside Character mapping.

FARMING WITH HERITAGE –THE CHALLENGE

There are many challenges in addressing the need to farm with heritage in mind. These include:

- Knowledge and understanding:

  - Awareness of site presence;

  - Advice and demonstration;

  - Building ownership and enthusiasm.

- Farming implications:
  - Reducing stocking;
  - Fencing out archaeological sites; and
  - 'No plough'? Minimum tillage?

CONCLUSIONS

It is important to develop a positive dialogue between the farming community and heritage conservation interests. In this respect the following are significant aspects:

- Language is very important:
  - Heritage interests need farmers as much as headlines and so a dialogue is important.
- Information – it is important to know what sites are and where they are, and to be able to communicate this effectively:
  - Location and management of priority sites and landscapes.
- Heritage legislation review – re-consideration of legislation and guidance is important:
  - How to turn negative messages to commercial advantage?
- Accepting change – on the one hand conservationists need to accept some change as inevitable in a dynamic landscape. Farmers also need to recognise the changing context and priorities of the farming industry. Increasingly they will have a role as positive custodians of the countryside and its heritage.

FARMLAND FLOWERS – THE IMPORTANCE OF CULTIVATION

Martin Harper
Conservation Director, Plantlife International

INTRODUCTION

Grasslands are under threat. In the UK:

- 95% of lowland meadows lost;
- Recent research suggests losses continue – conversion to cereal farming remains a problem.

AN INTRODUCTION TO PLANTLIFE:

- A charity dedicated to conserving all forms of plant life in their natural habitats, in the UK, Europe and across the world.
- 12,000 members, 22 nature reserves (3,900 acres = *c.*1,772 hectares).
- Lead Partner for 77 species, 400 Flora Guardians.
- Secretariat for *Planta Europa*
- We have offices in Salisbury, Bangor, Edinburgh and Bratislava.
- www.plantlife.org.uk

THE GLOBAL STRATEGY FOR PLANT CONSERVATION

- Adopted by the CBD at COP6 in April 2002, The Hague (Decision VI/9).
- To halt the destruction of plant diversity.
- The Strategy contains 16 outcome-oriented targets for 2010.

For the first time .....

.... we can measure the progress of the world's governments in protecting plant diversity.

RELEVANT TARGETS

- Target 5: assure protection of 50% of world's most important areas for plant diversity.
- Target 6: At least 30% of production lands managed consistent with the conservation of plant diversity.
- Target 7: 60% of the world's threatened species conserved *in situ*.

THE UK RESPONSE

- The UK response to the Strategy – Plant Diversity Challenge - is currently being drafted.

- This will contribute to the Johannesburg WSSD target of significantly reducing loss of biodiversity by 2010.

- Plant Diversity Challenge will set the agenda for plant conservation over the next seven years.

ARABLE FLOWERS

This group of plants has showed the greatest relative decline.

The decline of farmland birds has been highlighted in recent years. The decline of arable plants has been just as striking.

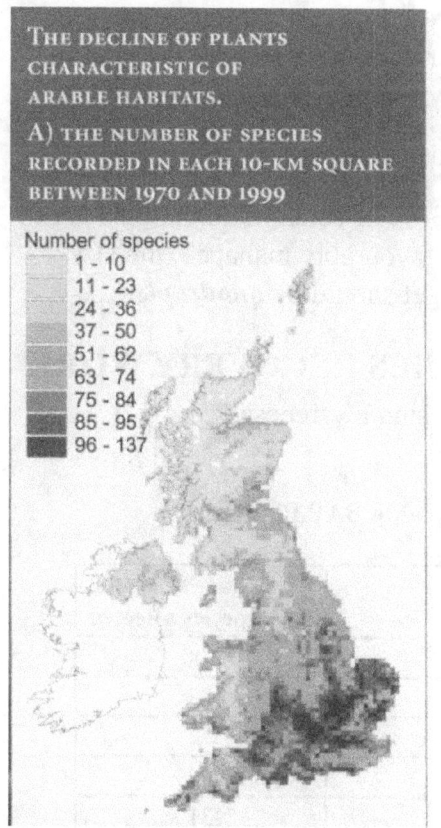

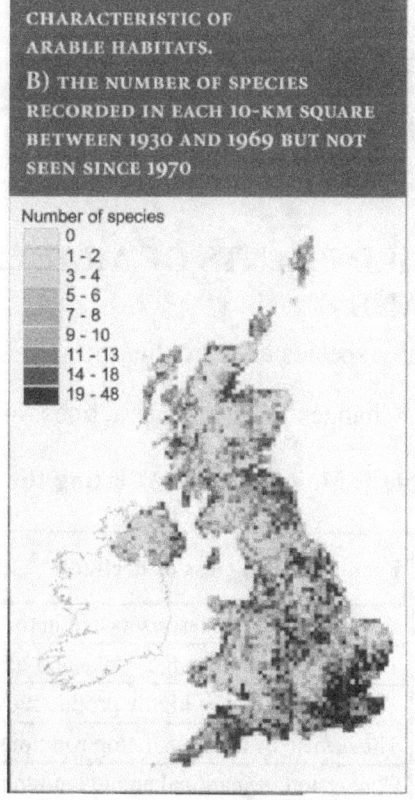

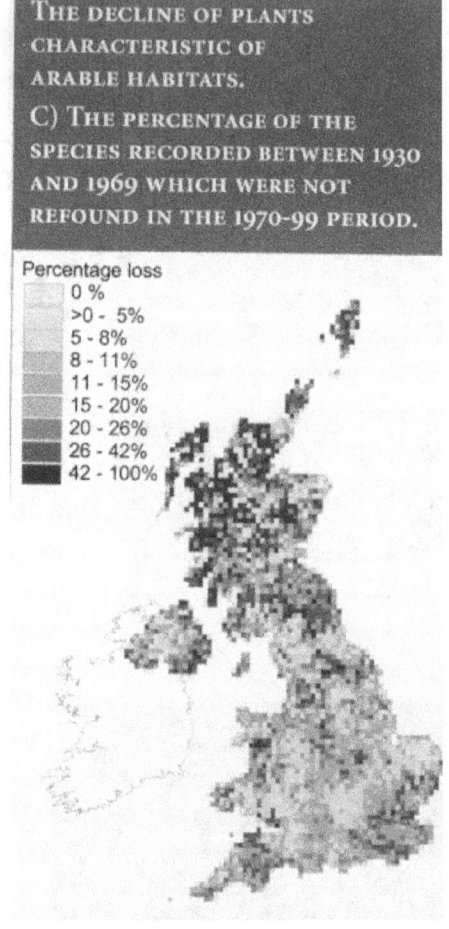

The decline of plants characteristic of arable habitats.
C) The percentage of the species recorded between 1930 and 1969 which were not refound in the 1970-99 period.

Percentage loss
- 0 %
- >0 - 5%
- 5 - 8%
- 8 - 11%
- 11 - 15%
- 15 - 20%
- 20 - 26%
- 26 - 42%
- 42 - 100%

WILD PLANTS OF ARABLE LAND

Many species are rare due to:

- Changes in farming practices; and
- Being regarded as weeds.

BIODIVERSITY ACTION PLANS

- Cereal Field Margins Habitat Action Plan.
- 13 species listed on UKBAP
- Each one with a 'lead partner' to drive and coordinate conservation action:
  - Plantlife lead partner for 10.
  - EN lead partner for 2.
  - Kew lead partner for 1.

CEREAL FIELD MARGINS TARGET

- Current target is 15,000ha in agri-environment schemes by 2010.
- This has been met, *but*
- if 30% of cereal field margins are to be favourably managed, the HAP target should be *quadrupled*.

SPECIES RECOVERY WORK

- Raising awareness.

Table 1: Major Factors Affecting the Loss/Decline of Arable BAP Plants.

Factor affecting loss or decline	Percentage of arable BAP species affected
Widespread use of fertilisers and herbicides.	100
The destruction of hedge-banks and other field-edge habitats.	85
The development of highly productive/competitive crop varieties.	77
The demise of traditional crop rotations.	69
Conversion of marginal arable land to pasture.	31
Abandonment of marginal arable land leading to a loss of beneficial ground disturbance.	23

- Organising volunteers / contractors.
- Practical on-site management.
- Guidance and support for site management and farming practices.
- Advising on site protection.

THE MANAGEMENT OF ARABLE LAND FOR RARER PLANTS

- Find out which arable flowers grow on your farm.
- Establish arable flower conservation areas, such as unsprayed headlands (arable flower margins).
- Cultivate and harvest arable flower margins at the same time as the rest of the field.
- Leave stubble as long as possible before ploughing next crop.
- Seek financial support for arable flower margins from agri-environment schemes.
- Do not use herbicides in arable flower conservation areas.
- Reduce herbicide use elsewhere, and only apply once advice has been sought to help protect arable flowers.
- Never apply fertilisers in arable flower conservation areas, and use lower rates elsewhere if possible.
- Avoid sowing a crop where arable flower conservation is being carried out, or sow just a very thin crop.

NEW ARABLE INITIATIVE: IDENTIFYING IMPORTANT ARABLE AREAS

- Collaborative project:
  - National agencies and organisations – EN, CCW, SNH.
  - NGOs – GCT, Northmoor Trust…
  - BSBI (Botanical Society of the British Isles).
  - CPA Agronomists.
  - FWAG farm conservation officers.
- Supported by:
  - Esmee Fairbairn Foundation; and
  - English Nature.

PROJECT AIMS

- Inventory of key sites – influence targeting of agri-environment schemes.
- Produce guidelines and management tools for farmers and agronomists.
- Increase awareness of this most threatened group of plants.

ACHIEVING PROJECT OBJECTIVES

- Recording presence of indicator species – by visiting agronomist or farm conservation officer.

- Follow up by a botanical recorder.
- Compilation of list of best sites.
- Use list to guide conservation efforts.

SUPPORT MATERIALS
- PDF & Hard copies:
  - Recording forms (and in Scotland insert);
  - ID booklet – species specific;
  - Courtesy letter – for the farmer.
- www.arableplants.org.uk

SUMMARY
- Two-stage surveys.
- Agronomist/ Farm conservation officer lead (or farmer).
- Information stored and used appropriately – owner confidentiality.
- Participation at all levels of detail welcome.

AGRI-ENVIRONMENT SCHEMES
- Entry Level Scheme.
- Higher-Tier Scheme.

Example Recording form

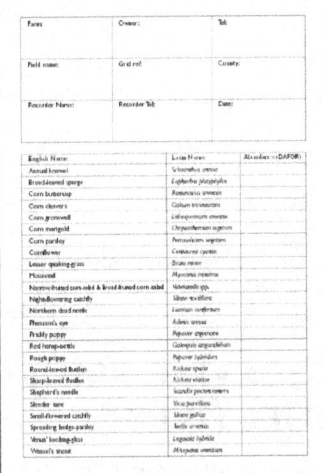

Mix of Government policy and market instruments needed - a pyramid of support

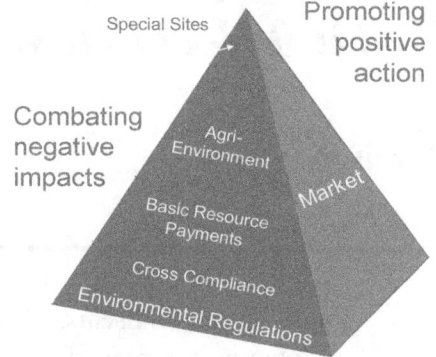

Support
+
Market
+
Advice
+
Research

Plantlife Contact

Amanda Miller
14, Rollestone Street
Salisbury, Wiltshire SP1 1DX
Tel 01722 342749
Email Amanda.Miller@plantlife.org.uk

WILDING BY DESIGN AS A FUTURE DRIVER FOR A NEW NATURE IN RECONSTRUCTING SOUTH YORKSHIRE'S FENS

Ian D. Rotherham and Keith Harrison
Sheffield Hallam University

ABSTRACT

Bordering North Lincolnshire, North Nottinghamshire, and South Yorkshire, the third largest fenland in England was almost totally destroyed by the early 1900s. The long-term impacts of intensified land management and particularly the drainage efforts of the Dutch engineer, Sir Cornelius Vermuyden, working for King Charles I, and then the renowned drainage engineer Smeaton, removed the wetlands from both landscape and memory. This paper addresses the consequences and impacts of these changes in the context of political and economic drivers for past change. The former extent of these wetlands was established as an outcome of the *South Yorkshire Biodiversity Research Programme*, field and archival research inform helping the creation of GIS computer maps of wetlands from pre-Roman times to the present day. Diverse sources have given insights into the lost fauna of this great wetland, and individual case studies show the past drivers for change.

The outcomes of this historical ecology research are being used to inform proposals to re-construct the wetlands in post-industrial and post-agricultural landscapes. The contemporary plans for restoration are justified by drivers such as water management (to resolve flood, drought, falling groundwater, and saline intrusion) and the need to foster rural economies through farm diversification. The political drivers include the idea of supporting the new rural economy through related leisure and tourism. There is also a need to comply with the EU Water Framework Directive, and to halt and reverse regional declines in biodiversity. There is also a move to justify new landscapes for carbon sequestration through wetland creation. The latter is in response to UK Government policy on climate change and is made more urgent by developments such as the new international airport at Finningley.

However, there are enormous barriers to change and issues arising from short-term approaches now being pursued. The lack of corporate vision and absence of ambition in key organisations is discussed. This is placed in context of a lack of awareness of critical issues in the scale of historic and prehistoric losses, and the consequent size of the task. This situation is further exacerbated by limited understanding of tourism and rural economics and the way in which the new landscapes will need to function, by many of those leading current changes. History demonstrates the relationships between landscapes, economy and society. It shows the need to generate landscapes that are sustainable and valued in every way including their social and economic functions. This is being achieved at individual sites and on a moderate scale. However, the challenge is to take the next step. Across the South Yorkshire and Lincolnshire Fens there is a possibility of an ambitious and successful restoration and re-creation of a sustainable and rich landscape, but failure to think big and broad is undermining the process.

INTRODUCTION

Rackham in *The History of the Countryside* (1986) suggested that "*about a quarter of the British Isles is, or has been, some kind of wetland*". On a similar theme in 2001 Chris Smout stated that: "*There are many thousands of hectares of what is now prime arable land, especially in northern England, that were in the 17th century, fen and mire*" and "*it is surprising how… Yorkshire.. fenlands have evaporated from general memory*". This paper considers the topic further and outlines the preliminary reconstruction of the historic wetlands. The research has generated the new observations and conclusions about the wetlands and the scale and effects of anthropogenic change, and these relate to images and perceptions of wetlands, especially bogs and fens that permeate the human psyche and influence attitudes. As Rod Giblett wrote in (1996):

"*Wetlands are not always, and for some not ever, the most pleasant of places. In fact they have often been seen as horrific places. In the patriarchal western cultural tradition wetlands have been associated with death and disease, the monstrous and the melancholic, if not, the downright mad. Wetlands are 'black waters'. They have even been seen as a threat to health and sanity, to the clean and proper body, and mind. The typical response to the horrors and threats posed by wetlands has been simple and decisive: dredge, drain or fill and so 'reclaim' them. Yet the idea of reclaiming wetlands begs the questions of reclaimed from what? For what? For whom? A critical history of wetlands' drainage could quite easily be entitled 'Discipline and Drain'.*"

By the early 1900s, England's third largest fenland, bordering North Lincolnshire, Nottinghamshire, and South Yorkshire was almost totally destroyed. It suffered from the long-term impacts of drainage by the Dutch engineers followed by intensive farming. Potential increased revenue was the driver for draining much of the lowland fens of England. In 1600 A.D., Parliament passed *An Act for the recovery and inning of drowned and surrounded grounds and the draining of watery marshes, fens, bogs, moors and other grounds of like nature*. The idea developed with James I and was implemented on behalf of Charles I. The build up to, and the impact of the drainage of Hatfield Chase are discussed in detail by Van de Noort (1997). Before drainage 36,420 hectares of the Humberhead Levels (De La Pryme, 1699), the area was '. *A continual lake and a rondezvous of ye waters of ye rivers ....*'

The research described here involved the mapping and 'virtual' re-construction of the former wetlands across South Yorkshire and adjacent areas. Fieldwork and archival research were used to help generate GIS computer maps of wetlands in the region. These were from pre-Roman to the present day. Furthermore, a range of sources was accessed to suggest the variety and abundance of likely fauna of these wetlands. This work is only in its infancy and just hinted at here, but is still remarkably revealing. Area-based case studies were used to identify the key political and economic drivers for change through history, and the consequences and impacts are discussed. The mapping process began with a consideration of key maps produced by earlier researchers. In 1933, Wilcox produced two maps that indicate the extent of prehistoric marsh, moss, and fen; one based on geological, topographical and climatic evidence, the other on early literature. Produced nationally they considered only the major lowland floodplains as historically wetland sites. However, the general approach was similar to that adopted for the present study.

Map 1. The Prehistoric wetlands of the region from Wilcox (1933)

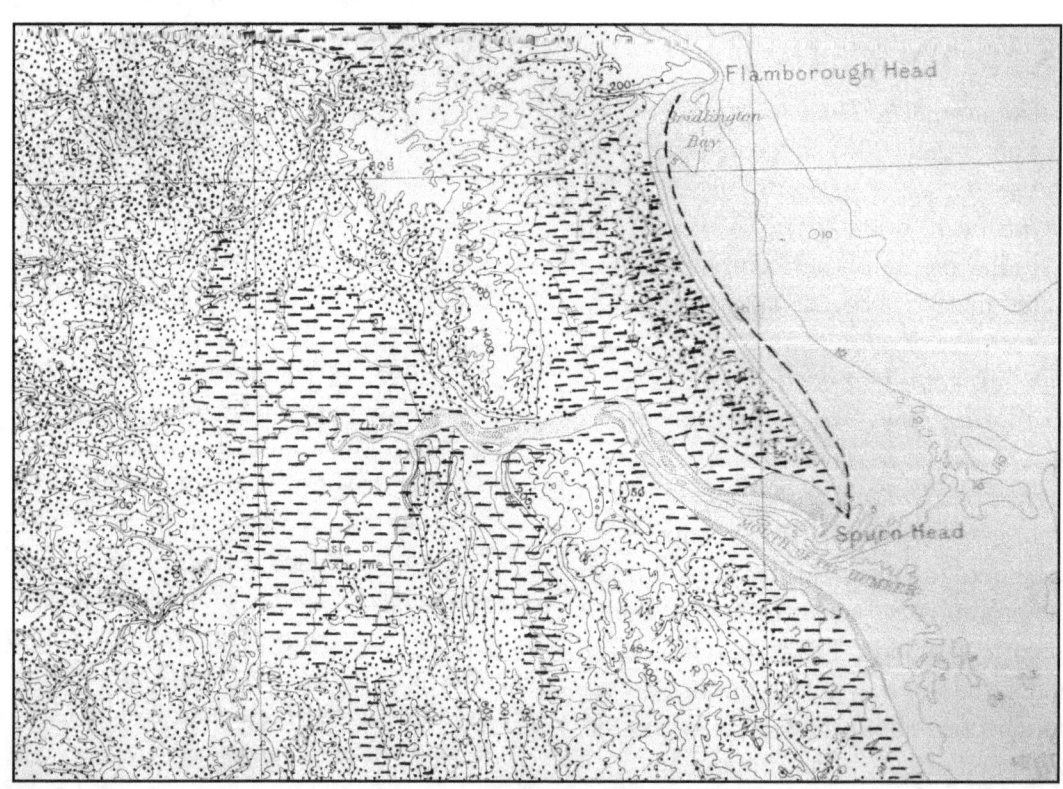

A further significant contribution to this type of research was the work Darby & Maxwell (1962) for the *Domesday Geography* series. They presented maps of the region with wetlands and related features such as peat and alluvium deposits, fisheries and mills. These maps start to assemble an image of the once extensive wetland landscape of the study area.

Map 2. The extent of wetlands from Darby & Maxwell (1962)

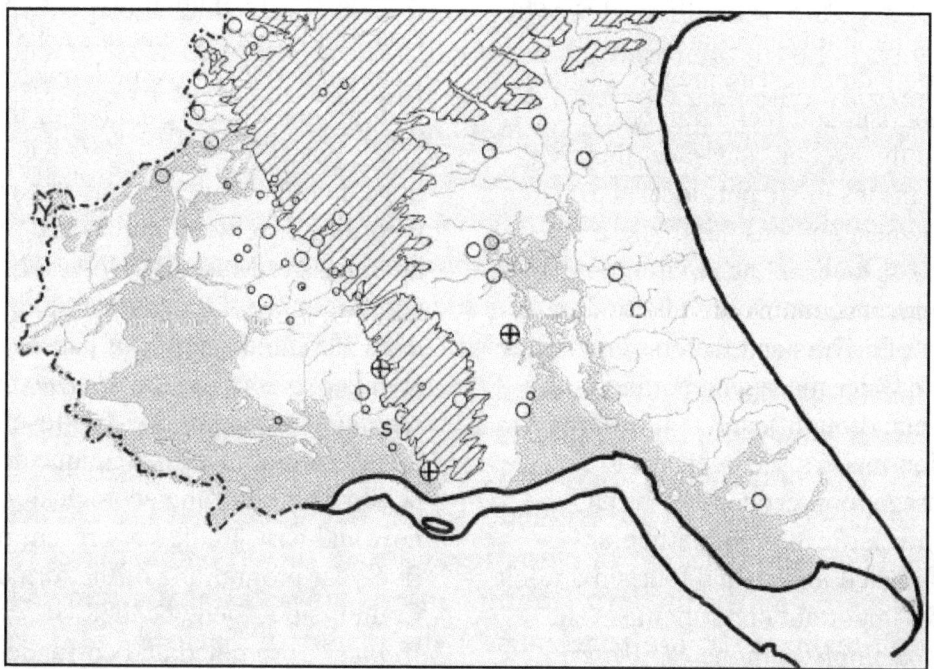

Map 3. The extent of wetlands, with peat and alluvium, from Darby & Maxwell (1962)

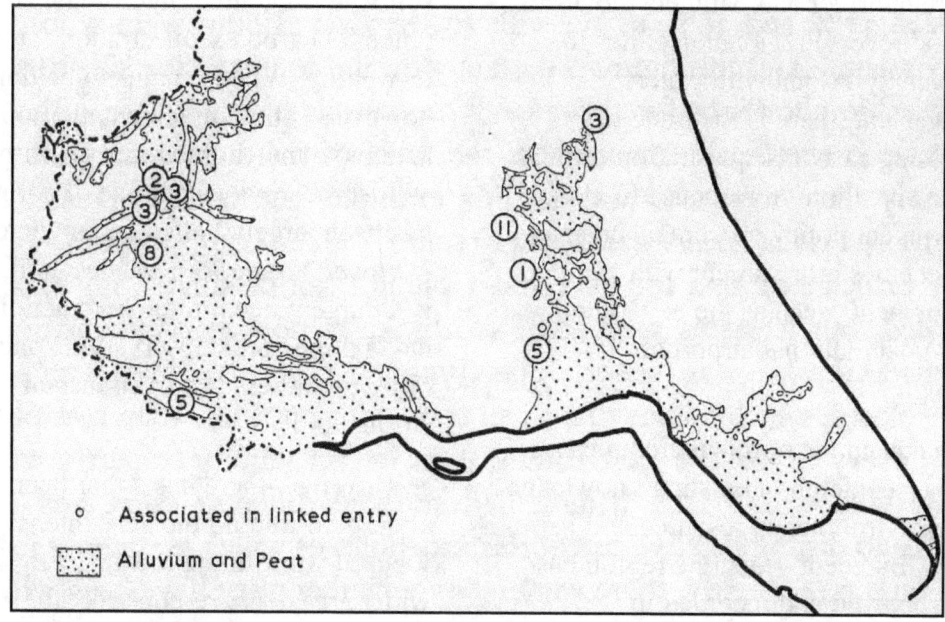

It is hoped that the research outcomes will help inform proposals to reconstruct the wetlands in the post-industrial and post-agricultural landscapes of this extensive region. In particular, there is interest in diversification of the farmed landscape and the agricultural economy with wetter conditions. The intention is that with tourism and recreation based around this wetter landscape, there will be the means to support local employment and business. These desired changes in the environment and in the local economy are justified by a matrix of drivers and factors. The issues include water management (and both flood and drought), and a desire by decision-makers and agencies to encourage rural economies through farm diversification. In particular, water-related leisure and tourism are felt to offer important opportunities. The need to comply with the *EU Water Framework Directive* is also an important driver and parallels moves to halt and reverse regional declines in biodiversity. Along with water management, there is the issue of addressing carbon sequestration through wetland creation. In response to UK Government policy on climate change this becomes more urgent with developments such as the new (early 2000s) international airport at Finningley.

An advantage of this regional case-study is the depth of existing knowledge of the environmental resource and its history. In recent years, the region has been surveyed and recorded in incredible detail. Van de Noort and Davies (1993), and Van de Noort and Ellis (1997) for example presented major reports on the findings of comprehensive archaeological studies across the Humberhead Levels and areas adjacent. In parallel with this, Buckland, and Whitehouse *et al.* (for example Whitehouse *et al.*, 1998; Buckland, 1979) have undertaken major and ground-breaking studies of the area's palaeo-ecology. There has been a huge amount of meticulous research and recording by entomologists and others at Doncaster Museum (Howes, Limbert, and Skidmore; for example Skidmore *et al.*, 1985), and a series of papers on the area is published as the *Thorne and Hatfield Moors Papers*. The result of all this work and more is a unique depth understanding of the ecological resource now and past. In the very recent past, a five-year programme of the former Countryside Agency called '*Value in Wetness*', promoted and co-funded detailed studies of land use, economics, soil water potential, hydrology, and potential carbon sequestration through re-wetting. What remains to be done however, is the implementation of actions to match this research output. Whilst the obvious decline of core areas has been largely halted and an extensive *National Nature Reserve* declared, there is an urgent need to move to actions beyond the core conservation zone in order to address critical issues of sustainability.

However, there has so far been no attempt to join up the very intensive and focused work in the lowlands, to the wider area, or to re-construct the landscape and ecological history of the region. In particular relationships between the lowland fens, bogs and heaths, the mid-ground of Coal Measure rivers and wooded valleys, and the extensive upper catchment of the south Pennines moors has been totally neglected. Furthermore, there has been no holistic attempt to draw together the information to present an interpretation of the historic landscape ecological resource. It is against this context that barriers to change and issues arising from short-term approaches and a lack of corporate vision are discussed.

METHODOLOGIES

A starting point for research was the early maps and accounts of the region. Then, in order to re-construct the extent and occurrence of wetlands across the Humber region, it was necessary to map evidence from topographic, geological and pedological sources, and from earlier maps. This approach follows that of Wilcox and of Darby, but then applies contemporary tools such as air photographs, remote sensing and the *MapInfo Geographical Information System* to create layers of landscape history. These were then constructed to show key changes in the wetland landscape. Rivers were mapped from *Ordnance Survey Geological Maps of Drift* (Ordnance Survey 1949-1969), and maps of the sixteenth to nineteenth centuries (Saxton, 1577; Saxton and Goodman, 1616; Vermuyden, 1626; Burdett, 1767; Jeffrys, 1772; Colbeck, 1782; Ordnance Survey First Edition). The distributions of alluvium were taken to imply original wetland, with over 100,000 hectares (over 1,000 sq. km.) identified. The preliminary results were then discussed with researchers interested in the region and knowledgeable about its landscape and ecology. Obvious anthropogenic change through construction of watermills, drainage for agriculture, urban expansion and industrial development, dumping of mine spoil, building of reservoirs, and transport systems, were incorporated into the maps. For a selection of specific areas, detailed case-studies of different parts of the river system were chosen. These had contrasting topographies. The historical review identified different drivers influencing the changed landscapes over time. The work then attempted to re-construct former wetland landscapes across the region, looking in detail at sub-areas and the chosen case studies. Time-sliced maps of former wetlands were produced. The final overview map covered the lowland and upland wet landscapes as one. The Humber fens are united through the Coal Measure valleys, with the south Pennine mires of the uplands.

RE-CONSTRUCTING THE FORMER LANDSCAPE ECOLOGY

The research aimed to do more than simply map the extent of wet landscapes and catalogue their loss. To understand the nature of these wetlands, it is important to both map their occurrence, and to reconstruct their former ecology. In order to do this, early accounts, itineraries and other sources such as feast menus and game books provide insight into ecology and use. This work is at a very early stage but still gives a glimpse into the historic wilderness. On-going research at Sheffield Hallam University, supported for several years by the former Countryside Agency, has scoped and assessed the potential for wetland-based nature- or heritage-tourism and recreation across the Humberhead Levels. This was to help guide a transition to a wetter landscape through the engagement of farmers and other landowners in policy-driven, but economically-facilitated diversification. This assessment gives a contemporary overview to the wetland landscapes of the region.

RESULTS

The study generated a series of computer maps of the original watercourses of the Rivers Don and Went, before the Roman Turnbridge Dyke (known to be Roman (Buckland, 2002)), and the first major anthropogenic change to the river system. This diversion captured the River Went and took part of the River Don into the River Aire. The Dyke may have been for the transport of goods and livestock, an extension from the Fens to Lincoln. Now confluent, these two rivers were once components of different river catchments. The locations of the better-known Thorne Mere, and two satellite meres were mapped; though it is likely that the region was dotted with other smaller, and now forgotten lakes, meres, carrs and pools. Vermuyden's map of the meres was used to locate the sites, though Taylor's study of the Old River Don, did suggest slightly different positions. In the wider landscape, extensive wetlands were suggested by maps of alluvial deposits

Map 4. A summary map to display the research findings

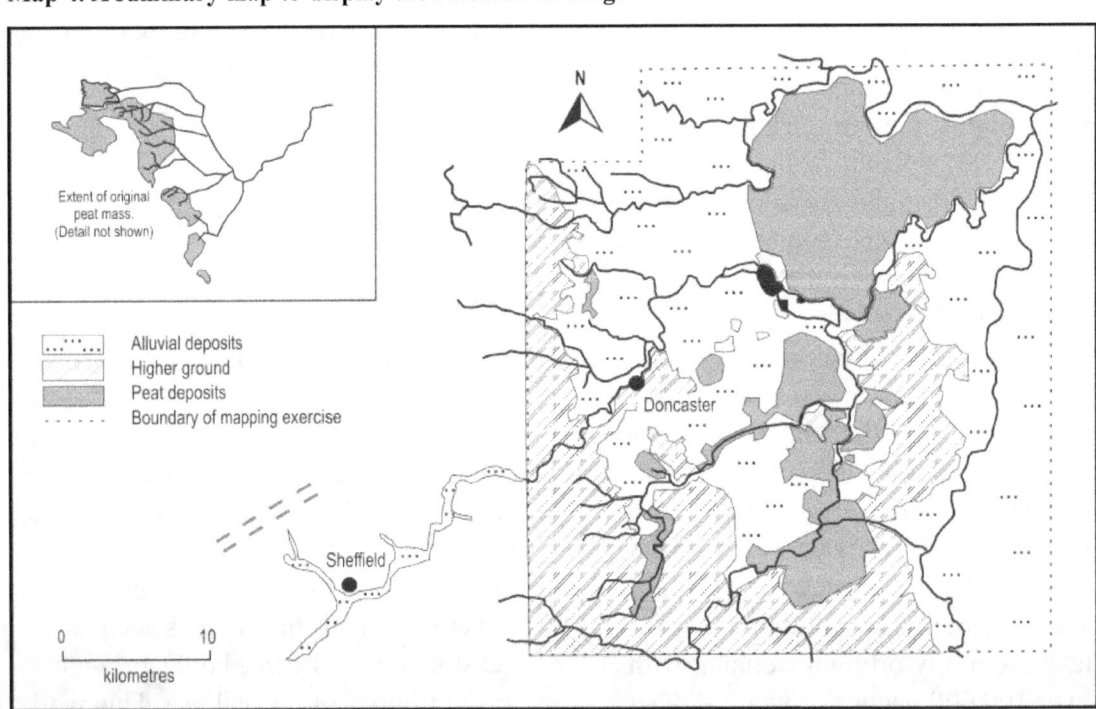

and peat and imposed onto the maps of the watercourses. The rivers and wetlands were shown in 1600, shortly before the major drainage works by Vermuyden and his colleagues.

Through the Dutch Drainage schemes, Thorne Mere was lost and the earlier course of the River Don was changed, diverting a number of major watercourses across the region (Taylor, 1987). The main driver for this change was improvement to agriculture, or at least the generation of capital from sales of land for agriculture. There may well have been other political motives in terms of subduing unrest and non-conformism at both regional and national levels. The extensive fens were always the refuge of independence and those seeking to distance themselves from the power of the state.

By 1800, the Turnbridge Dyke north of the Dutch River had gone (Jeffrys, 1772; Ordnance Survey First Edition), and Potteric Carr, south of Doncaster was drained in the late eighteenth century (Colbeck, 1782). Later phases of drainage in the nineteenth century were across the area west of the River Don, north of Doncaster; removing almost all the wetlands apart from remnants of peat on Thorne and Hatfield Moors. In the wider landscape of now intensive, mostly arable, farming, continued land improvement further desiccated the already dry lands. This period of intensive, agro-industrial farming has increasingly relied on groundwater abstraction for irrigation, in what is climatically a dry region, and at the same time, extensive land drainage to remove surplus water from this flat landscape. As most of the region is around or even below sea level, the sea is rising, and groundwater is falling, this is clearly not sustainable.

A FORMER WETLAND LOST FROM MEMORY

Anecdotal evidence from a wide variety of sources suggests that the area once teemed with wildlife, with birds, and probably mammals, in their hundreds of thousands. However, human impact has taken a major toll. Human predation was on a huge scale and peaked in the eighteenth and nineteenth centuries. In the earlier periods, in spite of the huge available resource, the impacts were limited by the technologies available for catching birds in open, wet landscapes. The advent of the Dutch Decoy and of effective fowling pieces changed all that. Hunting impacts declined through the nineteenth century. This was presumably because of almost total loss of wild stock and massive and widespread destruction of habitat. It is likely that improved availability of imported food was also a factor, as the commercial wild harvest was uneconomical, and that taken as of common rights became less worthwhile. However, despite the fall off in hunting, both commercial and sporting, the birds could not recover because of landscape change. We estimate that around 98% of the historic wetland was destroyed, and the 2% remaining would be altered beyond recognition.

Writing in 1895 Cornish described the carrs located south-west of Doncaster as outliers of the great fen originally extending north to the River Humber, east to the Trent lowlands, and south to Nottinghamshire. It included the Isle of Axholme, Thorne Waste, Marshland and Hatfield Chase fen. Pottric Carr was portrayed by Eagle Clarke (1887) as having vast numbers of duck, bittern, ruff and reeve, black-tailed godwit, marsh harrier, great crested grebe and water rail all breeding commonly up until the drainage in the late 1700s by Smeaton. Of all these changes it is perhaps Vermuyden's drainage of Thorne Moor and Hatfield Chase in the 1600s that is the best known. It is well documented, and with anecdotal evidence of a huge wetland resource; Taylor (1987) suggesting that the pre-Vermuyden landscape would have rivalled today's Coto Doñana in its wealth of birdlife. Chris Firth (1997) states: "*the destruction of the wetland habitats (here) would, by today's standards, be regarded as an ecological disaster of enormous proportions.... (that) could be argued as equal in proportion to the present day destruction of rainforests*".

However, the drainage of Thorne Mere and Hatfield Chase was only part of the scene of wetland destruction across South Yorkshire and the adjacent counties. In Yorkshire south of the confluence of the Ouse and the Trent, 70,000 acres of Hatfield Chase were constantly inundated before Vermuyden and his fellow Dutch undertakers commenced to drain it in 1626. At its heart was Thorne Mere, almost a mile over, and close by, Potteric Carr 4,000 acres near Doncaster. One of many outliers known as the Yorkshire Carrs, this fell to Smeaton and his engineers after a private Act of Parliament in 1764.

Records and memories of wildlife in the region give some impression of a long-vanished landscape. As noted by Smout (2000) the bittern was sufficiently common to have its own vernacular name and feature in local folk rhymes: '*When on Potteric Carr the Butter Bumps cry, The women of Bulby say summer is nigh*'. Still in the early 1900s, older people around Beverley recalled hearing the local bitterns. But for over two hundred years the pressure has been to tame the wilderness and to 'improve' the land. Cobbett in 1830 described the land reclaimed from the Humber area as the richest and most fertile he had seen in the whole of England outside the Cambridgeshire fenland. The efforts of the Dutch improvers increased the value of land at Hatfield Chase from 6d per acre to 10s. However, this value to the farmer and landowner does not reflect the full worth to the community living and working in and around the wetlands, before and after so-called 'improvement'.

A PRODUCTIVE LANDSCAPE

These wetlands provided fish, reed and rushes (for thatching, flooring and candles), peat fuel, brushwood from the carrs for fuel and light constructional work, and pasture for cattle. As Smout (2000) noted it was not only the marshes and meres of Yorkshire and

Lancashire that wetlands had economic value for people, but the same across northern Britain. Contrary to the views of many landowners and politicians at the times of improvement, these were rich and productive landscapes. This is reflected in the evidence of land use and productivity from a diversity of sources. These were important hunting lands, and from a very early date as evidenced by Conisbrough Castle park (South Yorkshire) which dates from around 600-700 AD (Colin Merrony pers. comm.). The hunting rights were presumably held by one of the Anglo-Saxon Earls. Then, from shortly after the Norman Conquest the 70,000 low-lying and often inundated acres of Hatfield Chase were the private forest of the de Warennes of Conisbrough, until in 1347, the Chase reverted to the Crown.

In 1607, the area held around a thousand Red Deer and Fallow Deer, described as once as common '*as sheep upon the hills*', and '*so unruly that they almost ruined the country*'. The last documented major hunt was in 1609. The royal hunting party in a hundred boats pursued five hundred deer across Thorne Mere (Jones, 1996). Hatfield Chase famous for its fisheries and swans, was disforested (1629) and drained in the 1600s. John Leland (Henry VIII's antiquary) gives an account of the feast for the enthronement of George Neville as the Archbishop of York in 1466. This may be exaggerated, and some of the food would be from the Derwent Washlands (north of our study area and south of York). However, the account provides a useful insight into likely wildlife and domesticated or semi-domesticated stock in the South Yorkshire and Humber marshes and fens at this time:

"Oxen 104; Wild Bull 6; Muttons 1,000; Veales 304; Porkes 304; Piggs 3,000; Kidds 204; Conyes 4,000; Staggs, Bucks and Roes 504; Pasties of venison cold 103; Pasties of venison hot 1,500; Swans 400; Geese 5,000; Capons 7,000; Mallard and Teal 4,000; Plovers 400; Quails 100 dozen; Fowles called Rayes 200 dozen; Peacocks 400; Cranes 204; Bytternes 200; Chickens 3,000; Pigeons 4,000; Hernshawes (young herons) 400; Ruff 200; Woodcock 400; Curlews 100; Pheasants 200; Partridges 500; and Egritts 1,000."

Reference to other regional household accounts confirms cranes, herons, snipe, bittern, quail, larks, dotterel, and bustards for the table (1526), peacocks, cranes, and bitterns (1530), and twelve spoonbills at 1s each, and ten bitterns at 13s and 4d (1528). Many of these are wetland birds and mammals from forest or chase. The accounts confirm that these were extensive and productive landscapes. It seems likely that little bittern, night heron, and purple heron probably survived in English wetlands until the 1600s. We know that cranes and spoonbills have been extinct as breeding birds in England for around 300 years. Ruff bred at Hatfield Chase until the 1820s, and Thomas Pennant in 1766 described the taking ruff in nets, fattening in captivity, and selling them for the table at 2s each.

In the relationship between people and nature in these wet landscapes, before modern guns were available, new techniques in wildfowling were important. In particular the Dutch Duck Decoy came in the 1600s, presumably with the Dutch drainage engineers. This made commercial exploitation of the resource effective and efficient. Each year thousands of wildfowl were captured from the South Yorkshire fens, Doncaster Corporation having a duck decoy as an investment or for the upkeep of the poor. Construction of the decoy and a special three-quarter mile embankment, 'Decoy Bank', to reach it cost £160. The circular decoy pond was 6½ acres of water with six 'pipes' to collect the ducks. The Decoy was let in 1662 for twenty-one years at an annual rent of £15. This fell in 1707 to only £3 per year maybe reflecting the impacts of drainage across the landscape and the contraction of the wetlands. In 1707 the lessee was specialising in pochards, one of the best ducks for the table. After settling on the water the birds were captured by nets raised with pulleys on poles. All the duck pipes were still there in 1778, but the last decoy man died in 1794. By the late 1800s the *Great Northern Railway* ran straight through what had been the decoy.

VALUE IN WETNESS and VALUE IN WILDNESS

Value in Wetness was the title of the regional *Integrated Land Management Project*, one of twelve such initiatives across England. The research outcomes from targeted and funded studies were intended to inform proposals to reconstruct wetland and wetter landscapes in today's post-industrial and post-agricultural scenario. There is particular interest in diversification of the farmed landscape and the agricultural economy to facilitate wetter conditions and a more sustainable future. Tourism and recreation are seen as potential economic drivers supporting local employment and business. In this way the local people and the business community can 'buy in' to the idea of re-wetting, and perhaps in re-wilding.

The changes in the regional environment and in the local economy have been influenced by a matrix of drivers and factors. Taking an historic perspective allows a longer-term appraisal of likely outcomes. Current issues include water management and in particular problems of both flood and drought. The need to comply with the *EU Water Framework Directive* is an important driver and parallels moves to halt and reverse regional declines in biodiversity. This combines with the desire by decision-makers and agencies to encourage rural economies through farm diversification. Water-related recreation and tourism offer important opportunities. Furthermore, along with direct issues of water management there is the potential of addressing carbon sequestration through wetland creation and wetter landscapes. At regional levels and in response to UK Government policy on climate change this has become more urgent. Developments such as the new international airport at Finningley make the situation especially acute. As noted earlier, there has been a huge amount of meticulous research most recently culminating in a five-year programme of the Countryside Agency called '*Value in Wetness*'. The latter promoted and co-funded detailed studies of land use, economics, soil water potential, hydrology, and potential carbon sequestration through re-wetting, to help draw together the earlier studies and provide an integrated vision for land-use change.

It is also interesting to note that whilst tourism and recreation, and specifically that related to wildlife and water, are seen as potential economic drivers for the region, plans for the major wetland nature conservation assets have no significant tourism input. There seems to be a lack of communication between conservation, tourism, and local stakeholders. In particular, this relates to the unique complex of Thorne and Hatfield Moors, but the issue is broadly applicable to most of the surrounding areas too. This is remarkable when the plans and proposals also include major visitor facilities. There is a serious problem of a lack of communication and indeed of a common language or purpose, between those managing the resources for conservation, and those seeking to promote the same for tourism and regional economic benefit. The situation has been similar with the major coastal managed retreat areas around the mouth of the Humber estuary, and in particular to the site of several hundred hectares at Alkeborough. (Of course coastal retreat has been re-badged as realignment, since this sounds less defeatist!) Here again there is tremendous potential to implement a major e-wilding scheme and to fully embed this in the local economy through local provenance foods from the nature reserve, and through tourism in relation to a wildlife spectacular. However, there seems as yet to be little prospect of this actually coming about. Local farmers were concerned that the desired breed for the marshes, the local Lincoln Reds was not sufficiently productive. But this is exactly why they are a good breed and the shortfall in income should be made up through the added value; local provenance foods, and the tourism revenue to the region. That is surely what joined up thinking is about. The environmental problems across the region are mostly linked to issues of over-intensive farming that is not sustainable, so to use this as a reason to not progress with the alternatives is very blinkered. There was even the possibility of grazing the area with a herd of Dutch Heck Cattle, but this was turned down.

So despite all these efforts, it remains surprising that so far there has been no attempt to either join up the very intensive and focused work in the lowlands, to the wider area, or to re-construct the landscape and ecological history of the region. Furthermore, there has been no holistic attempt to draw together the information to present an interpretation of the historic landscape ecological resource. It is also disappointing that from all these efforts there is still no sign of an effective and integrated approach applied across the region to address critical issues. At the same time, there is the potential here to re-wild and to re-wet on a massive scale to help address environmental issues and at the same time to kick-start a vibrant economy.

CONCLUSIONS

This integrated research approach provides an insight into historic drivers, and the barriers to change. These relate to two thousand years of human disruption of the ecosystem. The work shows that the research approach adopted, following the earlier studies of Wilcox (1933) is both valid and informative. The studies begin to demonstrate the former ecological richness of the region, a theme developed further elsewhere. However, there are major issues arising from short-term approaches and a lack of corporate vision.

The study draws on and acknowledges the work of others, in confirming the scale of wetland loss across the region. It presents evidence for the former extent of wetlands and wet landscapes across the study area. Importantly it demonstrates a continuity of wetland habitats spatially throughout the catchment, lowland areas linking along the river valleys to the upland blanket mires, and temporally at specific sites throughout centuries of change. The drivers for change have been noted and here are discussed briefly. For anthropogenic wetland loss, there has been a partial redress in the middle and upper parts of the catchment, through remnant millponds, later reservoirs, and more recently new wetland nature reserves. There are now subsidence flashes, flood management washlands, and purpose-built sites. It also seems increasingly likely that large wetlands will be developed across at least parts of the study area in years to come, and the recent works at RSPB Dearne Valley and on-going at YWT Potteric Carr Nature Reserve are evidence of this. But there is a problem in that all these areas are but a tiny fraction of the once extensive and varied wetland. There is no evidence of a wider approach or that there is any real awareness as yet of the scale of historic loss, and therefore the enormity of the task that lies ahead.

This study was in parallel with work on potential tourism to the area, and on farm and landscape diversification. Interestingly the multi-agency sponsored research on the future of these wet landscapes specifically ignored the *Water Framework Directive*, and the implications of on-going strategies for major managed floodlands for flood alleviation. Both have significant policy and economic implications for future management of these wetlands. Indeed it seems strange that in seeking to address a complex of economic and political drivers to resolve deeply embedded problems, some of the main forces at work can be overlooked. This has to undermine any serious conclusions in terms of positive action. In an historic perspective too, it seems that concerns about droughts and water shortages, and about floods and widespread inundation last so briefly in the political mind. A similar experience is occurring with UK rural policies that followed the *Foot-and-Mouth Crisis*. Blink and its gone! The crises that punctuate the socio-economic and political landscape, and hence shape the altered environmental resource seem to result in a flurry of funded and directed research and policy initiatives. These can gather significant information, as in *Value in Wetness*, and may support or promote some modest achievement on the ground. However, in this case it is likely that the major project would have happened in any case, and are at best isolated beacons of light is an otherwise unchanged landscape of decline. There is as yet little sign of any of the changes at a wider landscape scale that will be necessary to avert further, serious long-term decline in the resource. What is more, there is no indication from politicians or leading bodies such as Development Agencies that they understand let alone are willing to address, the challenges they face. It is generally 'business as usual', and that focuses on short-term economics, jobs, and passing references to 'sustainable development' and 'quality of life'. The latter are acceptable as long as they don't impinge on the former! The attempts at 'greening' are in many cases a veneer that is by definition skin deep. The huge challenges and the depth and breadth of truly joined-up thinking, are only just being realised. In the meantime opportunities are being lost. What is more, these opportunities should be at the very core of sensible and long-term sustainable regeneration. With global environmental change there will, in a few decades, be no choice.

This corporate myopia is not good, and does not give cause for optimism. With global climate change and atmospheric carbon dioxide identified as a major causal agent, the massive drainage of wetlands and wet landscapes must have been a factor. A major contributor in the to carbon release in the past it has left a legacy of hugely modified hydrology today. For the Humberhead Levels, Hogan and Maltby (2005) considered the potential for carbon sequestration in the wetlands. They noted that carbon sequestration can be effective as one of a range of measures to bring down atmospheric carbon dioxide levels. They suggested a strategic approach to wetland conservation and management can be effective in this. The approach should deliver other social, economic, and environmental benefits too. Importantly in terms of strategic planning, they note that freshwater restoration across key parts of the area could make the biggest contribution to carbon sequestration. Coastal inundation for example, would be relatively ineffective in this respect. They highlight the need for a broad strategic response to carbon issues, especially in relation to projected increase in air travel etc. This is a particularly pertinent for this region. During the course of the study, the new *Robin Hood (Sheffield and Doncaster) International Airport* came into being at Finningley. So far, there has been no attempt to mitigate or moderate any adverse environmental impacts (including carbon dioxide) by any positive action at any level, political, strategic, or otherwise. There are

Integrated Catchment Management Plans, and *Catchment Abstraction Management Plans* from the Environment Agency, but these are not multi-disciplinary in terms of joining up with initiatives such as *Value in Wetness*. Furthermore, they consider the whole catchment (the upland zone above the supply / balancing reservoirs is ignored in models), or the history of change across the region.

It is suggested that a more holistic approach should be informed by knowledge of change at a landscape scale over the last two thousand years. This broader vision is necessary if the future challenges are to be effectively addressed. Failure to engage more fully in this approach will lead to continual under-achievement. There will be rhetoric but little action in terms of environmental restoration and remediation at the scale required, in water management, and in a wetland-based tourism revival of the rural economy. It is absolutely clear that much of the contemporary intensive farming in the lowland region is environmentally unsustainable. This is discussed elsewhere. However, to resolve deep-seated issues of centuries of land drainage and 'improvements', requires farmers to 'buy into' a new approach, and without their co-operation further progress will be slow. The future vision needs to incorporate bold and large-scale reversion to wetlands, and conversion of a wider landscape to wetter farmland. Farming diversification and tourism combined can provide economic drivers, but if the tourist and recreational visitor are to become the economic consumers of these newly wetter landscapes, there needs to be a strategic vision with effective funding. Above all, it needs to actually happen rather than just being talked about. The long term future of this landscape will be wetter and wilder, and it would be as well to anticipate this rather than react respectively and too late.

REFERENCES

Anon. (1990) *Reprint of the First Edition of the One Inch Ordnance Survey of England & Wales, Sheet 22, Doncaster*. David & Charles Publishers Ltd

Buckland, P.C. (1979) *Thorne Moors: a palaeoecological study of a Bronze Age site; a contribution to the history of the British insect fauna*. Department of Geography Occasional Publication No. 8, University of Birmingham, Birmingham.

Buckland, P C (2002) *South Yorkshire Wetlands - the palaeo-ecologist's view*. South Yorkshire Wetlands – a one-day workshop on wetland biodiversity and management, Sheffield Hallam University, November 2002. Sheffield Hallam University. *South Yorkshire Wildlife Review* (In press).

Burdett (1767) *Map of the County of Derbyshire*. Derbyshire County Libraries, Matlock.

Colbeck, J. (1782) *Plan of the rivers cuts drains and watercourses subject to the direction of the Trustees and which drain and preserve certain Lands within the parishes Townships and Hamlets of Doncaster Balby Carhouse High Ellers Bessicarr Loversall etc.* Local Archives, Doncaster MBC Libraries.

Cornish, C.J. (1895) *Wild England Today*. Seeley and Co., London.

Crossley, D. (Ed.) (1989) *Water Power on the Sheffield Rivers*. Sheffield Trades Historical Society & University of Sheffield, Sheffield

Darby, H.C. and Maxwell, I.S. (Eds.) (1962) *The Domesday Geography of Northern England*. Cambridge University Press, Cambridge.

Director General of the Ordnance Survey (1949-1969) *Geological Survey of Gt Britain (England and Wales*: Ordnance Survey.

Sheet 77 Huddersfield, Drift, 3rd Series, 1949

Sheet 78 Wakefield, Drift, 3rd Series, 1962

Sheet 79 Goole, Drift, 7th Series, 1967

Sheet 86 Glossop, Drift, 3rd Series, 1951

Sheet 87 Barnsley, Solid With Drift, 3rd Series, 1951

Sheet 88 Doncaster, Drift, 7th Series, 1969

Sheet 99 Chapel-en-le-Frith, Drift, 7th Series, 1967

Sheet 100 Sheffield, Solid And Drift 1956, 6th Series

Sheet 101 East Retford, Solid And Drift, 1967, 7th Series

Environment Agency (2002) *LIDAR Map of the Lower River Don Catchment*. Environment Agency North East Region

Firth, C. (1997) *900 Years of the Don Fishery: Domesday to the Dawn of the New Millennium*. Environment Agency, Leeds.

Giblett, R. (1996) *Postmodern wetlands, culture, history, ecology*. Edinburgh University Press, Edinburgh.

Hadfield, C. (1972) *The Canals of Yorkshire and North East England Volume 1*. David & Charles, Devon.

Hadfield, C. (1973) *The Canals of Yorkshire and North East England Volume 2*. David & Charles, Devon.

Hogan, D.V. and Maltby, E. (2005) *The potential for carbon sequestration in wetlands of the Humberhead Levels*. Royal Holloway Institute for Environmental Research, Royal Holloway University of London, London.

Jones, M. (1996) *Deer in South Yorkshire: An Historical Perspective*. In: Jones, M., Rotherham, I.D. and McCarthy, A.J. (Eds.) (1996) *Deer or the New Woodlands? The Journal of Practical Ecology and Conservation, Special Publication*, **1**, Wildtrack Publishing, Sheffield.

Jeffrys (1772) *Map of the County of Yorkshire*. Harry Margary, Lympne, Kent (1973).

Linton, D. L. (Ed.) (1956) *Sheffield and its Region - A Scientific and Historical Survey*. British Association for the Advancement of Science.

Rackham, O. (1986) *The History of the Countryside*. J M Dent & Sons, London.

Rotherham, I. D. (2002) *South Yorkshire's Wetlands - their obscure past and uncertain future*. South Yorkshire Wetlands – a one-day workshop on wetland biodiversity and management, Sheffield Hallam University, November 2002. Sheffield Hallam University. *South Yorkshire Wildlife Review* (In press).

Saxton, C. (1577) *Map of the County of Yorkshire*.

Saxton, C. and Goodman, W. (1616) *Map Of Pottrick Carr near Doncaster*. Local Archives, Doncaster MBC Libraries.

Skidmore, P., Limbert, M. and Eversham, B.C. (1985) The Insects of Thorne Moors. *Sorby Record*, **No. 23**, Supplement.

Smout, C. (2000) *Nature Contested - environmental history in Scotland and Northern England since 1600*. Edinburgh University Press, Edinburgh.

Taylor, M. (1987) *Thorne Mere and the Old River Don*. Ebor Press.

Umpleby, T. (2000) *Water Mills And Furnaces On The Yorkshire Dearne And Its Tributaries*. Wakefield Historical Publications.

Van de Noort, R. and Davies, P. (1993) *Wetland Heritage: an archaeological assessment of the Humber Wetlands*. Humber Wetlands project, University of Hull, Hull.

Van de Noort, R. and Davies, P. (1997) *Wetland Heritage of the Humberhead Levels: An Archaeological Survey*. Humber Wetlands project, University of Hull, Hull.

Vermuyden, C. (1626) *Map of Hatfield Chace Before The Drainage*.

Whitehouse, N.J., Dinnin, M.H., and Lindsay, R.A. (1998) *Conflicts between palaoecology, archaeology and nature conservation: the Humberhead Peatlands SSSI*. In: Rotherham, I.D. and Jones, M. (Eds.). (1998) *Landscapes --- Perception, Recognition and Management: reconciling the impossible?* Proceedings of the conference held in Sheffield, UK, 2-4 April, 1996. *Landscape Archaeology and Ecology*, **3**, 70-78.

Wilcox, H. A. (1933) *The Woodlands and Marshlands of England*. University Press of Liverpool, Hodder & Stoughton, London.